Manuel Zapata Olivella

AND THE

"Darkening"

OF

Latin American Literature

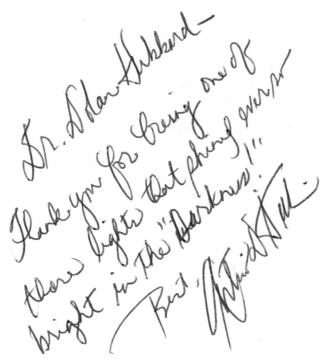

Dr. Dolan Hubbard—

Thank you for being one of
those lights that shines
bright in the "Darkness!"

Best, [signature]

Afro-Romance Writers

This series is intended to promote scholarship on black writers of
French, English, Portuguese, and Spanish expression from the
Americas and Africa.

Series Editors

MARVIN A. LEWIS
M. J. MURATORE

Manuel Zapata Olivella

AND THE

"Darkening"

OF

Latin American Literature

ANTONIO D. TILLIS

University of Missouri Press

COLUMBIA AND LONDON

Library of Congress Cataloging-in-Publication Data

Tillis, Antonio D.
  Manuel Zapata Olivella and the "darkening" of Latin America
literature / Antonio D. Tillis.
      p. cm. — (Afro-romance writers)
  Includes bibliographical references and index.
  ISBN 0-8262-1578-5 (alk. paper)
  1. Zapata Olivella, Manuel—Criticism and interpretation.
2. Blacks in literature. I. Title. II. Series.
  PQ8179.Z38Z88 2205
  863'.64—dc22   2005008092

♾™This paper meets the requirements of the
American National Standard for Permanence of Paper
for Printed Library Materials, Z39.48, 1984.

Typesetter: Crane Composition, Inc.
Printer and binder: Thomson-Shore, Inc.
Typeface: Baskerville MT

TO

current and future scholars/researchers in the field of Afro-Hispanic studies,
this volume is respectfully dedicated.

TO

Doc, Professor Marvin A. Lewis,
for his continued belief in my possibilities as a scholar/educator

TO

my aunt Geraldine Aldridge
for her unyielding support, confidence, and love.

AND

In loving memory of my mother,
Bettye Jean Tillis

CONTENTS

ACKNOWLEDGMENTS

I wish to acknowledge the following for their contributions to this project: Marvin A. Lewis and M. J. Muratore, the Afro-Romance Writers series editors; the Afro-Romance Institute for Languages and Literatures of the African Diaspora at the University of Missouri–Columbia, the School of Liberal Arts dean's office at Purdue University for providing funds through the Dean's Incentive Grant and Matilda Stokes for her assistance. All translations in English are my own.

ABBREVIATIONS

The following abbreviations have been used in the text:

Changó, el gran putas	*Changó*
En Chimá nace un santo	*En Chimá*
China 6:00 a.m.	*China*
Las claves mágicas de América	*Las claves*
Hemingway, el cazador de la muerte	*Hemingway*
He visto la noche	*He visto*
Pasión vagabunda	*Pasión*
La rebelión de los genes	*Rebelión*
Tierra mojada	*Tierra*

Manuel Zapata Olivella

AND THE

"Darkening"

OF

Latin American Literature

INTRODUCTION

The literary work of Afro-Colombian writer Manuel Zapata Olivella explored in this study is best characterized as the postcolonial literary "history" of people of African descent and the socially dispossessed in the Americas; hence, the "darkening" of thematic content and of a majority of his protagonists and antagonists. His works disclose literary "realities" that mimic twentieth-century struggles of blacks, the poor, and the downtrodden. In consequence, it is important to understand that the cultural, social, political, and economic textual circumstance has a genesis dating back to the arrival of the first Africans in the New World. Thus, in order to better understand this author and his works, it is incumbent upon readers and scholars to explore briefly the historical continuum which Manuel Zapata Olivella's thematic foci reflect.

As documented in works by scholars such as Franklin Knight, Herbert Klein, Darién Davis, Leslie Rout, and others, the history of Africans in Latin America is said to have begun in 1502, when Christopher Columbus first brought Europeanized Iberian Africans to the shores of the New World.[1] For the next four hundred years, the history of Africans and their descendents was to be as conflicted as the ever-increasing population. Historical accounts attest to the early "diversity" in social status of the first African population to arrive. Categorized as "ladinos," "bozales," and free Africans, the issue of their social positionality and legal status resulted in much trepidation.[2] Early European tribunals debated this concern, resulting in the adoption of codes and other legislations that reflected the vacillation in ideology regarding this population.

---

1. For a detailed historical account of the African in the New World, consult Franklin W. Knight, *The Caribbean: The Genesis of a Fragmented Nationalism* (New York: Oxford University Press, 1990), Herbert S. Klein, *African Slavery in Latin America and the Caribbean* (New York: Oxford University Press, 1986), Leslie Rout, *The African Experience in Spanish America: 1502 to the Present Day* (Cambridge: Cambridge University Press, 1976); and Darién J. Davis, ed., *Slavery and Beyond: The African Impact on Latin America and the Caribbean* (Wilmington, Del.: SR Books, 1995). Additionally, *Africans in the Americas: A History of the Black Diaspora* (New York: St. Martin's Press, 1994) by Michael L. Conniff and Thomas J. Davis offers valuable historical insights.

2. "Ladino" refers to an Iberianized African, one who is socialized in the traditions of Spain and Portugal prior to arriving to the New World. "Bozal" generally is the antithesis, referring to an African subject that has not been assimilated.

The fifteenth-century African "problem" for the European crown centered on how Spain, Portugal, and other imperial nations were to socially situate or "classify" these colonized and enslaved subjects. This early historical account foreshadowed issues pondered by generational tribunals regarding the social integration of Africans; the debate continues today.

An important factor affecting the African was the declining and dying indigenous population, which provided the first source of free "manual labor" required by the first European invaders. As the law of supply and demand dictated, the need for an increase in human capital escalated with developments in mining, agriculture, and other industries. The steady decline in the indigenous population required the establishment of an alternative labor pool. The African, because of many factors such as adaptability to land and labor demands, became the plausible substitute. Thus, the history of the introduction of the African onto the soil of the New World is marred by indecision regarding civil status, exploitation, marginalization, vilification, and terrorism.

For the literary production of Manuel Zapata Olivella, this history provides ripe material on which to base the thematic focus of a majority of his works. The history of people of African descent in his native Colombia is similar to the historical experience suffered by blacks in other parts of the Americas. Slavery, oppression, marginalization, silencing, and historical racism, all of which are themes explored in the works of Zapata Olivella, characterize this existence. Borrowing from Colombian historical moments, Zapata Olivella embellishes, with regard to Africans and those of African ancestry, the generational marginalization and disenfranchisement of this population. His published works reveal the denial of a historical presence. His texts address the blatant absence of contributions of Afro-Colombians to the development of the nation. Additionally, this writer of mixed heritage painstakingly deals with the history of miscegenation and race-mixing influencing the cultural and ethnic milieu of Colombia today. If not for his contributions to Latin American letters, Colombian letters in particular, lost from the recorded chronicle would be the voice of hundreds of thousands who have, since the sixteenth century, called this South American nation *la patria*.

In today's context, it is quite exhilarating that the works of Afro-Colombian writer Manuel Zapata Olivella are beginning to find readers in literary circles outside his native country. In the United States, scholars are finally recognizing his merit as they assess over five decades of his literary accomplishments. At an open forum in 2002 at Purdue University, I was pleased to note that Canadian scholar and former president of the Modern Language Association Linda Hutcheon did not limit her remarks to the well-known *Chambacú, corral de negros* (1967), *En Chimá nace un santo* (1963), and *Changó, el gran putas* (1983). Hutcheon's expanded references to Manuel Zapata Olivella, along with those to other black writers in Latin America, were announced in conjunction with an upcoming project on Afro-Hispanic literature. As groundbreaking as this endeavor might have appeared to some scholars in attendance, the names of Zapata Olivella, Nelson Estupiñán Bass, Candelario Obeso, Adalberto Ortiz, Arnoldo Palacios, Pilar Barrios, and a host of others are already well known to a growing group of predominately African American scholars who have been publishing on these and other Afro-Hispanic writers. One is Hutcheon's Canadian colleague, African American scholar Richard Jackson, who has spent much of his academic career in Canadian universities. Jackson reigns as a major pioneer in Afro-Hispanic studies. His contribution to Latin American literary history is his diligent focus on the national and international contributions of marginalized writers in Latin America. In his 1979 study of black writers in Latin America, Jackson focuses on the ideological development of the literary trajectory of many of the early literary figures in Spanish America of African descent, Zapata Olivella among them. Additionally, in 1997, Jackson notes: "Manuel Zapata Olivella, the dean of black Hispanic writers, is making his way into both the Hispanic and Western literary canons."[3]

Jackson's assessment reflects the attitude of many Afro-Hispanic scholars. The global range of his thematic focus provides an international flavor to his works that contributes to his reputation as an international man of letters. Social and political issues of geographical spaces figure prominently in his novels. In *China 6 a.m.* (1955), his focus is communist China. With *He visto la noche* (1949), *¿Quién dio el fusil a Oswald?* (1967), and *Chambacú*, emphasis is placed on the United States. *Changó* transports the reader through several continents as the narrative voice moves through Africa, the United States, South America, and the Caribbean. Thus, this author's broad geographical-thematic literary scope extends his appeal well beyond Colombia and Spanish America.

Also to his credit is his literary flexibility. Manuel Zapata Olivella is

3. Richard L. Jackson, *Black Writers and the Hispanic Canon* (New York: Twayne, 1997), 51.

not only a novelist, but also an essayist, dramatist, and short story writer. Many of his works have received national and international recognition through literary prizes and awards. In consequence, many of his novels and critical essays are being translated into English, French, and other languages, allowing readership of this gifted author to expand beyond the confines of the Spanish-speaking world. In addition, the second generation of Afro-Hispanic literary scholars (those being mentored by Afro-Hispanic pioneers such as Richard Jackson, Marvin Lewis, Miriam de Costa-Willis, Ian Smart, Dellita Martin-Ogunsola, and others) is focusing its scholarly work on this author discovered by the academy in the 1970s. This continuity of scholarship, in addition to the continuing publications of Zapata Olivella, attest to the importance of this writer and his emerging reputation in the canon of literary masterworks.

A Brief Biography of Manuel Zapata Olivella

In *Black Writers in Latin America* (1979), Richard Jackson documents the development of literary blackness as an aesthetic in the writings of certain Latin American writers. Jackson begins his analysis with the noted Cuban poet Nicolás Guillén. He positions Guillén as one of the earliest twentieth-century writers in the Spanish Americas to employ this aestheticism in his literary work. From Guillén, Jackson progresses chronologically, suggesting Afro-Colombian Manuel Zapata Olivella as the best example of a mid-twentieth-century writer of African ancestry in Spanish America whose narrative focus centers Afro-Latin American realism. Twenty years after that assessment, Jackson refers to Zapata Olivella as "the dean of black Hispanic writers," a distinction that the life and works of this talented writer and humanitarian continue to exceed.

Researching the life of Manuel Zapata Olivella would require treading over many continents in search of facts and historical anecdotes. This writer of mixed African, indigenous, and Spanish descent has created a corpus of literary works that exemplifies his eclectic nature and moves beyond theoretical limitations of conventional travel narrative. His longevity and impressive list of multigenre works have inspired many young Latin American writers of African descent, who regard him as the generative source of their literary heritage. Additionally, his theories on the ideologies of race/ethnicity in Latin America have served as the literary and personal bedrock for many of these emerging Afro-Hispanic voices.

Hailed by Marvin Lewis as "one of Colombia's leading men of letters," Manuel Zapata Olivella was born on March 17, 1920 in Lorica, Colombia to Antonio María Zapata and Edelmira Olivella and died at his home in Bogotá on November 19, 2004, at the age of eighty-four.[4] His ethnic heritage, which becomes a major point of reference in his latter works, results from historical miscegenation and slavery in the New World. His father was a black-identified mulatto and his mother was Creole (half-Spanish and half-Indian). For the maturing writer, the need for a self-defined identity plagued much of his literary discourse. In his texts, Zapata Olivella introduces the reader to the mélange of "subjectivities" that define his personhood. As mentioned above, he speaks of his mother as being *criollo* and his father as *mulato*. In his attempt to situate his identity between those poles, he enters into that ambivalent space that defies categorization. A close reading of his works reveals that the process of identity construction and racial classification constitutes a major preoccupation with these ideologies. Thus, in the evolving attempt to negotiate his personal identity, Zapata Olivella reconfigures himself as tri-ethnic, creating an amalgam of his ethnic heritages that encompasses the composition of both parents. He contends that the issue of identity reconfiguration is shared by many Latin Americans who desire to understand the complex meaning of "self" in order to celebrate and embrace the richness of their collective identity.

Formal education was a necessary component in the life of Manuel Zapata Olivella and his five siblings. Their father, Antonio María Zapata, received a degree from the University of Cartagena; he was the university's first black-Colombian graduate. Ciro Alegría recounts in the prologue to Manuel Zapata Olivella's first published novel, *Tierra mojada* (1947), that the senior Zapata dabbled in writing: "His father enjoyed reading and was even accustomed to writing one or more articles, one or more short stories." (Al padre le gustaba leer y hasta solía escribir uno que otro artículo, uno que otro cuento. *Tierra*, 8) Alegría notes that Antonio María Zapata produced a series of short stories that were well received by a foreign literary magazine. As a result of their father's influence, Manuel and his brothers and sisters received a formal education and became promulgators of Colombian culture through literature and folklore. In a footnote in the prologue to *Tierra*, Alegría

---

4. Marvin A. Lewis, *Treading the Ebony Path: Ideology and Violence in Contemporary Afro-Colombian Prose Fiction*, 85.

mentions in an editorial note that his eldest brother, Antonio Zapata Olivella, received second place in the Colombian novel competition in 1942 for his unpublished novel, *Trivios bajo el Sol* (Junctions beneath the Sun). Continuing the tradition that had been established by their father, another brother, Juan Zapata Olivella, in addition became a noted poet-dramatist, and his sister Delia, a well-regarded folklorist.

Manuel Zapata Olivella's academic career was abruptly disrupted. He entered the University of Bogotá as a medical student after completing secondary education. He soon abandoned his medical studies due to financial pressures and a desire to explore the world. For the next few years, with more curiosity than money, he journeyed throughout the Americas and traveled to Europe. In the prologue to *Tierra,* Alegría recounts some of adventures of the Colombian *pícaro* as he journeyed from Colombia to Panama, Costa Rica, Nicaragua, Honduras, Guatemala, Mexico, and, finally, the United States. Interestingly, the anecdotes shared with the reader are important markers on the author's road to maturity both as a man and as a writer. Alegría tells of the author's encounters with U.S. troops in Panama, his experiences on a banana plantation in Costa Rica, his posing as a Cuban boxer in Guatemala (earning enough money to travel to Mexico). The Peruvian writer also mentions the hardships encountered by Zapata Olivella while in Harlem that led him to the doorstep of Langston Hughes. Many of these adventures are likewise chronicled in the writer's own works.

During this period of "discovery," Manuel Zapata Olivella began his career as a writer. His numerous adventures provided the raw material from which his works were constructed. In 1944, he returned to the University of Bogotá to complete his medical training, which he accomplished in 1949. Zapata Olivella's academic hiatus exposed him to the world and to himself. The pause allowed this anthropological writer to journey throughout the world collecting "qualitative data" from multicultural encounters that would serve as the foundation for future literary production.

As a writer of fiction, Zapata Olivella compares favorably to the most industrious writers of world literatures. Between the 1940s and the 1990s, Zapata Olivella published over a dozen novels. Additionally, he wrote a number of critical essays and short stories during this time frame. His novels include *Tierra, He visto, Pasión vagabunda* (1949); *China, Hotel de vagabundos* (1955), *La calle 10* (1960), *Detrás del rostro* (1963), *Cham-*

bacú, En Chimá, ¿Quién dio el fusil a Oswald? (1967); *Changó, El fusilamiento del diablo* (1986), *Levántate mulato* (1990) and *Hemingway, cazador de la muerte* (1993). His major essay collections are *Nuestra voz* (1987), *Las claves mági-cas de América* (1989) and *La rebelión de los genes* (1997). This publication record attests to the author's dedication to his craft, as do the literary prizes he received in honor of his innovative literary techniques.

A number of intellectual and literary figures directly influenced the personal and professional development of Manuel Zapata Olivella. Yvonne Captain-Hidalgo mentions many such influences who were in-strumental in shaping Zapata Olivella's stylistic and thematic develop-ment:

> The nineteenth-century poet Candelario Obeso and the twentieth-century anthropologist Rogerio Velásquez are two Afro-Colombians who contributed to Zapata's sense of the worth of his everyday culture and of the microcosmic world of the Afro-Colombian and his daily strivings. Writers like the Indigenist Ciro Alegría and the post-Indigenist José María Arguedas contribute to his focus on the political aspects of the downtrodden. At the same time, they help to widen his circle of thematic repertoire to include other racial and cultural groups.[5]

There was yet another individual who would greatly affect the life of Zapata Olivella: the reigning prince of the Harlem Renaissance, Lang-ston Hughes. In a published interview with Zapata Olivella, Captain-Hidalgo questions the author regarding his relationship with the esteemed poet and records his early admiration for the writer, his desire to meet Hughes, how he came to meet Hughes, and the long friendship that en-sued.

Zapata Olivella is no stranger to the American academic community. In the 1970s, he was a visiting professor at the University of Kansas, where he taught courses in Colombian literature and culture. Since the 1970s, he has lectured widely throughout the United States, frequenting conferences and colloquia at major universities such as Howard Univer-sity and the University of Missouri–Columbia. He has presented papers at numerous international symposia on a wide variety of topics such as African and Colombian folklore, African diaspora literature, race/ethnic-ity in the New World, and the evolution of Colombian literature.

---

5. Yvonne Captain-Hidalgo, *The Culture of Fiction in the Works of Manual Zapata Olivella*, 9.

Manuel Zapata Olivella has garnered numerous prestigious literary prizes both in and outside of his native Colombia. One of the earliest was the Spanish Premio Espiral, awarded in 1954 for his dramatic work *Hotel de vagabundos*. In 1963, he received a literary prize for *Chambacú* from the well-regarded Casa de las Américas in Cuba as well as the National Prize for Literature for *Detrás del rostro* in Bogotá. For *Levántate,* Zapata Olivella was awarded the prestigious Parisian Human Rights Prize in 1988. In 1989, he received the Simón Bolívar Prize in Bogotá for his radio broadcasts on Colombian identity. In 1995, Manuel Zapata Olivella was deemed *Caballero de las Orden de las Artes y la Cultura* (Gentleman of the Order of Arts and Culture) in Biarritz, France. The accolades for his literary accomplishments attest to the regard for his work on a global scale. In Colombia, his acclaim as an important national (and international) writer is being recognized. In 2000, the minister of culture sanctioned a reprinting of his *Pasión* and *He visto* as a singular work as a national tribute to the writer. The minister of culture bestows such honor to Colombians who have made invaluable cultural contributions. With this honor, *Pasión* ranks among the most well-regarded literary texts in Colombia. Additionally in 2000, Manuel Zapata Olivella was one of eight Colombians honored by President Andrés Pastrana Arango, so designated as the "Generation of 1920." The most recent of the potential international honors is his nomination in 2002 for the prestigious Príncipe de Asturias literary prize in Spain. Again, this nomination is of great significance not solely because of its international prestige, but for the fact that the nominator was the Fundación Punto Literario located in his birth town, Lorica. It is to be expected that the prizes and awards with which he will be honored in the future will continue to be among the most distinguished. It is my belief that he is a future contender for the Nobel Prize for Literature.

Manuel Zapata Olivella held many political posts within the government of his native Colombia. His most recent appointment was to the Colombian embassy in Trinidad, West Indies, where he served from 1998 to 1999. His highest ranking diplomatic post was first secretary at the Colombian embassy in Trinidad. The fact that he was a scholar, writer, and diplomat committed to the advancement of Colombian culture and governance is indisputable. His life's trajectory attests to such a commitment.

Until his death, Zapata Olivella resided with his wife in Bogotá, where he continued to engage in scholarly activity, contributing articles to many academic journals. In the past he traveled widely, presenting thought-provoking lectures at conferences, lecture series, and symposia around the world. Failing health had curtailed extensive travel, yet he remained vibrantly engaged through this writing. His brother Juan Zapata Olivella is the sole survivor of a family of writers. The literary baton is passing to his daughter Edelma Zapata Pérez, who in 1999 published her first work, a volume of poetry, entitled *Ritual con mi sombra*. Thus, the spirit of revolutionary, writer, scholar, and Afro-Colombian bestowed on him by his father, is witnessed in the work of the offspring of one of Colombia's most celebrated authors, Manuel Zapata Olivella.

Chapter I

Tierra mojada

The Genesis of an Africanized Literary Trajectory

Tierra mojada (1942) begins the literary trajectory of Manuel Zapata Olivella, Afro-Colombian medical doctor, scholar, anthropologist, and one of the most gifted writers of the Spanish-speaking African diaspora. In an earlier study, I suggested that this novel shares many features of the Latin American regionalist text as defined by scholars. These essential characteristics include a narrative focus centering on the complexities of a specific geographical region and the treatment of relationships between humankind and the identified environment. Central to these texts are a number of "natural" challenges presented within the novel. I observed further that Zapata Olivella's initial novel is emblematic of *la novela de la tierra* in Spanish America because of its thematic representation of the "land" and the sustained focus on human interaction and coexistence with it. I argue that despite the chronological limitations used to identify the regionalist novel in Latin America, the thematic leitmotifs typically ascribed to the Latin American regionalist novel (principally the emphasis on the relationship between the land and the inhabitants of the region) can be found in works extending decades beyond this literary movement's presumed ending point.

Prior to engaging in a philological discussion of the text, it is important to understand the peculiarities of the geographical "place" presented in *Tierra*. When Manuel Zapata Olivella published his first novel, Colombia had not reached the same level of postmodern, unified nationhood as many other Latin American countries. Numerous works produced in Colombia during the 1940s and 1950s thematically reflect the regional aesthetic of a particular region or neighborhood. This serves as a justification for the myopic regionalist perspective found in *Tierra*. The novel concentrates on the narrow topographical confines of the Sinú River valley. In this regard, Raymond L. Williams clarifies Colombia's geographical complexity:

. . . Colombia was essentially four "nations" (or semi-autonomous regions) for at least a century, approximately from the 1830s to the midtwentieth century. The nation's political, economic, social and cultural history supports this proposition. By the 1850s these regional divisions had taken form, finding increased definition throughout the remainder of the nineteenth century. Regional demarcations remained firmly intact during the first third of the twentieth century and begin to disintegrate after the 1930s with the modernization process. Symbolic dates for the beginning and the end of this "nation of regions" would be 1830 to 1958, from the collapse of the first Colombian supraregional unity to the National Front.[1]

In a historical survey spanning more than a century, Williams articulates the complexities of regionalism in Colombia by its historical legacy of four quasi-independent nations. Such acknowledgment lends credence to the longevity of a regionalist focus in Colombian literature. From the 1830s to the 1950s, the territory referred to today as Colombia evolved from four semiautonomous regions: the Interior Highland, the Coastal, the Greater Antioquian, and the Greater Cauca. Each region constituted a self-sustaining, mini-nation and exhibited its own distinct representation of "Colombian" cultural reality. Due to the elongated existence of separate "regions" in Colombia and the complexity of regionalism as a literary movement in Latin America, it is not inconceivable that Zapata Olivella situates *Tierra* within the confines of Colombia's Sinú River valley in order to capitalize on this region's cultural and ecological configuration. To this end, Raymond Williams argues:

Colombia's geographic conformation has been a key factor in the development of the nation's regionalism. The mountain ranges of the three cordilleras have posed enormous obstacles to any kind of unity. Interregional transportation, economic activity, communication, and cultural activity have always been challenging and frequently nonexistent. Rather than looking to a neighboring region or its capital, the Colombian who has turned outward has traditionally been more likely to look abroad. . . . The tobacco merchant of Ambalema (a small town in the Magdalena River valley boarding Cundinamarca and Tolima) of the 1850's had more economic contact with German merchants in Bremen than with, for example, capitalist merchants in Medellín or Cali.[2]

1. Raymond L. Williams, *The Colombian Novel: 1844–1987* (Austin: University of Texas Press, 1991), 12–13.
   2. Ibid., 13–15.

The explication provided by Williams underscores the internal difficulties thwarting the creation of a national infrastructure as well as the external influences that fortified regional traditions in Colombia. Colombia's attempt to achieve national unity was thus problematized by this diversity. The lack of collective, national governance created many obstacles toward efforts to achieve a national body of "representative" literature. As Williams points out, in order to move toward statehood, unifying institutions, such as a national transportation system and interregional communication, would be necessary to link the four regions, which were geographically separated by river valleys and mountain ranges. Of the four delineated regions of Colombia, the Coastal region provides the setting for Zapata Olivella's *Tierra*.

Zapata Olivella presents the theme of man's constant struggle to survive within the ever-changing, yet unyielding forces of nature. Land and nature constitute unnamed protagonists in this work when the Correa family struggles to manipulate geographical space for its own well-being. Essential to the development of the plot is the unwillingness of the people of the Sinú Valley to change or destroy their ecological surroundings. Nature in *Tierra* is a force confronting man in this Colombian region as well as an essential element to his survival. Gregorio, Próspero, Jesús, and their compatriots understand that their salvation is tied to the land and to nature. Consequently, their collective goal is not to conquer nature, but to create a possibility for coexistence. In *Treading the Ebony Path*, Marvin Lewis affirms that *Tierra* focuses on the real and ever-present struggle of the *campesinos* against the natural ecological occurrences that unequivocally regulate the course of the inhabitants: "As a work of art, *The Drenched Earth* is certainly not 'mysteriously inspired.' It is an interpretation of social perceptions, based on the fictional representation of characters and circumstances, and, as such, represents the manner in which the author views the continuing struggle of the *campesinos* of the Sinú River Basin."[3] Zapata Olivella's first published work novelistically displays this intimate relationship between man and nature and offers the reader a glimpse of the realities of life in one of Colombia's quasi-independent regions.

The plot centers on a struggle between antithetical forces: the oppressor and the oppressed. The oppressor is the black land-hungry rancher, Jesús Espitia, who has acquired his land and wealth through

3. Lewis, *Treading the Ebony Path*, 94.

the exploitation of the rice plantation workers. He is portrayed as a ruthless "master" who has no regard for those who till the land and cut the rice. The narrative voice presents him as one who is totally ignorant of his African ancestry and who exhibits a hatred of self that he projects onto poor blacks and others who work for him. The oppressed are represented by the family of Gregorio Correa, in particular the family's patriarch, el viejo Goyo.

In *Tierra*, Manuel Zapata Olivella provides the reader with an insider's view of family life in Los Secos from the vantage points of the oppressed and the oppressor. The depiction of the oppressed Correa family reveals the customs and traditions that are endemic within this Colombian region. The patriarchal social structure identifies Gregorio as the embodiment of the "head of the household." Consequently, his status and standing within the family endows him with great responsibilities and autonomy. The father is the sole decision maker of the unit, acting on behalf of its members, consistent with the image of the Latin American machista-type. Gregorio makes decisions relative to his household with little or no input from other members. He displays his affection for his children by leading his son, José Darío, into manhood by example. His relationship with his daughter, Rosaura, is one of love and concern. Gregorio is emblematic of the illiterate, uneducated rice farmer of the Sinú. His main objective, like that of all oppressed people, is to escape the exploitative hands of Jesús. When dispossessed of his property, he packs his family and remaining possessions into a canoe and heads out in search of more amenable surroundings. He is depicted as a strong-willed man who is determined to survive the opposing forces of nature and the tyranny of Jesús in his quest to create a better life.

As a husband and father, Gregorio's concept of responsibility reflects the conventional and sexist ideology of masculine privilege. He displays his love for his family through work, by his efforts to provide for them. In an attempt to care for his family, Gregorio leaves his ranch in San Bernardo and ventures into the mouth of the river basin. His family includes a wife, Estebana Seguro, characterized as being of indigenous origin, one son, and one daughter. Estebana suffers from rheumatism and relies on popular medicine to alleviate the pain. She is thus depicted as the resident medicine woman, whose remedies are emblematic of her "tribal" heritage and constitute a rejection of "official" medical practices. However, it is also true that the river basin as well as the socioeconomic situation of the family compel Estebana to hold true to her inherent dependence on the land for her physical well-being. Through the characterization of Estebana, Zapata Olivella's narration accomplishes three primary objectives. First, it gives the reader insight into the role and positionality of the distinct group of women who reside in the Sinú River basin. Second, it reinforces the economic plight of the Correa family, when Estebana is presented lacking the financial means to seek "official" medical attention if desired. Her narrative portrait is that of a rustic woman who struggles to survive with her family as they navigate the waters of the Sinú in search of a better existence. Third, it uses Estebana to "color" the story in regards to race/ethnicity. As mentioned earlier, she is described as being Indian and employing popular cultural practices.

Gregorio and Estebana's offspring, Rosaura and José Darío, manifest the hardships of life on a *champa,* or raftlike canoe, constantly relocating as their family is displaced by floods, storms, and the complexities of life on the river. Rosaura, like her mother, battles illness; her health has deteriorated from exposure to the elements and the conditions of the region. She suffers from malaria and oftentimes is fever-ridden and close to death. José Darío strives to emulate his father, whom he views as strong and worthy of his admiration. An additional member of this family is their loyal dog, Mocho, who shares in the family's afflictions. Other important characters of the novel include Próspero Huelva, a dear friend of Gregorio; his son, Vinicio; Jesús Espitia, the mulatto oppressor of the region; his son, the "Mono"; María Teresa, the fiancée of José Darío; and Manuel Olivares, the revolutionary schoolteacher. These characters are important to the development of the plot as they create intricate love triangles, shift power paradigms, and bring to life the complexities of region.

By concentrating on the institution of family, Zapata Olivella constructs a fictional representation of traditional patriarchal family structure, where men are breadwinners and are responsible for the physical labor and the financial well-being of the household. Women are relegated to childbearing, childrearing, and other domestic obligations. The story depicts the countless challenges facing the people of the region, such as hunger, the frequent lack of money, and the scarcity of food. Interestingly, these hardships serve to reiterate their dependence for survival on the land and nature:

Family life in Los Secos developed within the tightest of limits, everything being by hand: the stove, the bed and the roosters, who in the evenings with their song, longed for the lost meadows. Until then, only the housing problem had been solved. Fishing, in part, relieved the hunger; lines were cast at all hours and food was not lacking, but it was necessary to complement meals with other ingredients.

(La vida familiar en Los Secos se desarrollaba dentro de los más estrechos límites, estando todo a la mano: fogón, cama y los gallos, que en las tardes solían añorar con su canto las perdidas praderas. Hasta entonces solo se habían resuelto el problema de la vivienda. La pesca, en parte, aliviaba el hambre; se flechaba a todas horas y no faltaban alimentos, pero era necesario complementar la comida con otros ingredientes.) (*Tierra*, 77)

Physical labor is an integral part of daily life for the dwellers of Los Secos. The narrative voice describes the region as one where the essence of man's existence is in almost every respect tethered to land and nature. His nourishment as well as his financial gain is tied to both. Los Secos emerges as an agricultural community where the male members cultivate rice, the major staple in the region and the primary source of income. Nature emerges as a controlling force in the outcome, as success with the land depends wholly upon her cooperation. Life is a series of intense manual labors: collecting heavy timber, tilling the land, planting rice seeds, cultivating the crops, harvesting them and hauling them off for sale to "gringos" oftentimes at prices far below their actual worth:

From morning to night they would cut and haul the heavy wood in order to receive the lowest possible price that the gringo would set. In the evenings, after a long journey through the bay, they returned with their canoes to Los Secos where the women and children awaited them. The money earned, as little as it was, relieved their hunger and raised their spirit.

(De mañana a tarde cortaban y acarreaban los pesados leños para recibir el precio bajo que imponían los gringos. En las tardes, después de un largo recorrido a través de la bahía, regresaban con sus champas a Los Secos, en donde los esperaban las mujeres y los hijos. El dinero ganado, por escaso que fuera, aliviaba el hambre y fortalecía el espíritu.) (*Tierra*, 77)

For the families surviving in Los Secos, "life ain't been no crystal stair." The narrative voice recounts the people's endless battles for survival as they strive to overcome the challenges that threaten their very existence.

Through the depiction of the Corea family's fight against the oppressive forces against them and their struggle to survive in the midst of the unpredictable behavior of nature, the inhabitants of the Sinú River valley epitomize the reality of life in this particular region.

Of significant importance to the development of the plot is the land, *la tierra*. It functions within the text as a major component in understanding the region and those who inhabit it. For the dwellers of the Sinú River valley, survival depends on their relationship with the land. Antonio Francisco Anillo Sarmiento, in one of the earliest dissertations dedicated to the work of Zapata Olivella, underscores the bond between man and the land he cultivates: "In the second chapter, that which is objectified for us is the union of man and land: the desire, intensely felt, of having a plot of American soil where one can settle and by scraping the fertile surface, obtain that which gives us the nourishment that our bodies need."[4] Anillo Sarmiento reaffirms a basic factor regarding man's dependency on the land: it provides a food source and gives access to ownership and region-nation status. Marvin Lewis and Anillo Sarmiento both take note of the dual purpose of land and nature as represented in the text: both a taker and a sustainer of life. Commencing with the initial chapter and progressing throughout the work, the reader is engaged constantly with the terrain of the valley and learns quickly that the land's primary role is to provide man with his physical and economic survival. The waters "baptize" the reader into the bleaker reality that nature can give as well as take life.

That Zapata Olivella reveals an intimate attachment to this region is not surprising. The brief biographical sketch included in this study reveals that Zapata Olivella is a "son" of the Coastal region. Reiterating the sense of "connectedness" between the two entities, Ciro Alegría states:

> A novelist is always a walker of souls and regions, who at times explores them with his plants and others with his pen. Many are able to do both and those like Balzac are few who simply "made-up his mind to explore." This is how Zapata Olivella was, who had known already his native areas and the region of the Sinú by traveling to the Amazon forest. In the Meta river, a hurricane taught him how houses were moved from one side of the river bank to the other.

4. Antonio Francisco Anillo Sarmiento, "La novelística comprometida de Manuel Zapata Olivella," 154.

(Un novelista es siempre un caminante de almas y regiones, que a veces las explora con sus plantas y otras con la pluma. Muchos hacen ambas cosas y son raros los que, como Balzac, solamente "sentáronse a caminar." Es así como Zapata Olivella, que ya se tenía conocidos sus lares nativos y la región del Sinú, marchóse a la selva amazónica. En el río Meta, un huracán le enseñó la forma de mudar casas de la orilla a la otra.) (*Tierra*, 8–9)

As Alegría suggests, Zapata Olivella is no stranger to the area depicted in his work or to the catastrophes plaguing the fictional characters of this Colombian region. As Alegría notes, he experienced hurricanes and the ecological destruction of the Meta River, something which enables him to render a verisimilar portrayal.

Zapata Olivella's use of description is effective in centering the readership within a particular geographical space and its unique characteristics. Common to the area are devastating storms that cause diluvial destruction. Swamps, marshland, and river valley topography are vividly described along with native creatures such as regional birds and animals like the "mochuclo," "churri-churri," and "manatí." This regionalistic "coloring" can be found in subsequent works by Zapata Olivella, where topographical landscaping is symbolically converted into geographical symbols of "place."

Another regional/geographical perspective presented in *Tierra* is the connection between racial categorization and social class. The author exposes the challenging life of poor Afro-Colombian river dwellers, whose ethnic origin and racial composition contribute to their social positioning. Additionally, as the two social constructions of race and class are opposed, an even greater complexity is revealed: the vilification and exploitation of those of African descent in this Colombian region, an observation emphasized by Anillo Sarmiento:

It consists of a principle narration where the social problem of the black Colombian is presented to us as being in the personalities that stand out like "the old Goyo" who embodies the virtues of the oppressed man of color and the personality of Jesús Espitia, representative of the mulatto exploiter that abhors his black blood and as a means of advancing his life, intensifies the exploitation of the darker-skinned people.[5]

5. Ibid., 153.

According to Sarmiento, *Tierra* set the stage for what will become a major thematic focus in Olivella's work: the social marginalization of Afro-Colombians. The racial composition of the people of the Sinú River valley and the role "race" plays in their interaction emerge as central trends in this early novel. The complicated issue of race in a space where its definition is blurred becomes problematized with the juxtaposition of class. Through characters such as the mulatto Jesús Espitia, Zapata Olivella explores the theme of black self-hatred. Many Latin Americans of African ancestry often try to efface blackness through economic mobility or a hyperbolic valorization of "non-black" components of their mixed heritage. Jesús Espitia thus becomes emblematic of the complex issue of race and class in Latin America where many racially/ethnically mixed Latin Americans attempt to emulate and embrace the prevailing ideal based on mainstream acceptance and social privilege. The text clearly reveals passages that are race and ethnicity specific, thereby expanding the borders of the Sinú to include Latin America as a whole:

> In the hollow of the river, fixed to the defense of the port, the canoes were piling up to the sun. In the middle of the market, the men were coming and going like ants in a huge job of harvesting. Some showed their Spanish mestization, that in its toil of conquest stayed pure or mixed. Melancholy aborigine faces, that contrasted with the roguish look of blacks and mulattos, were not scarce.

> (En la hondonada del río, sujetas a la defensa del puerto, las champas se hacinaban al sol. En medio de la mercadería los hombres trajinaban como hormigas en una gran labor de recolección. Algunos revelaban el mestizaje hispano, que en su afán de conquista quedóse puro o mezclada. No escaseaban los rostros aborígenes con acentuada melancolía que contrastaban con la mirada pícara de los negros y mulatos.) (*Tierra*, 128)

> Gregorio's body highlighted his blackened skin next to Prospero's dry and rusty skin, who was Indian, without realizing it. His buddy, a mulatto, was also ignorant of his African ancestry. They were mere country men, born and raised on the banks of the Sinú.

> (El cuerpo de Gregorio relucía su alqui-tranada piel al lado de la seca y mohosa de Próspero, que era indio, sin saberlo. Su compradre, mulato, también ignoraba su ancestro africano. Ellos eran simples campesinos nacidos y criados a orillas del Sinú.) (*Tierra*, 22)

As is evident in the citations above, the tapestry of this region is woven from fragments of history. The mixture of peoples whose blood is laced with remnants of an indigenous, African, and Spanish ancestry constitutes a literal "body politics" chronicling the history of racial mixing in the region. But as Marvin Lewis notes, this racial and ethnic delineation in the novel is not solely for the purpose of literary aesthetics. Rather, it represents the novelistic adaptation of a perceived reality: the link between social status and pigmentation. The narration presents a social structure where those of lighter hues are elevated to positions of presumed superiority over those of darker shades. Jesús offers an example of a darker-hued man attempting to "invade" or be assimilated into the space of the light-skinned by means of economics. The reality is that his wealth, albeit acquired through exploitation, is not adequate to "lighten" the burden of his African ancestry.

This notion of social determinism based on shades of blackness is pervasive in the text and complicates the existence of Gregorio and his peers. Even more interesting is the fact that Zapata Olivella tries to blind these characters to such realities, causing the reader to take even more note of the prejudice. The novel establishes a caste system of color gradation that is intimately connected to social position, creating a power paradigm based on race and pigmentation. Consequently, characters in the novel are victimized by the concepts of light-skinned privilege/superiority and the need for ethnic whitening. This is accentuated through the literary manipulation of Jesús Espitia and his "adopted" son, the Mono, who is treated as "white." Consequently, the ambivalence of identity is emphasized through characters who lack a real sense of self-consciousness. The complex and contested definition of racial and ethnic identity in Colombia is seen as emblematic for all Latin America. Zapata Olivella literally reconstructs the social hierarchical order in his work in order to expose the "silenced" complexities of race and ethnicity. This promotion of agency becomes a characteristic narrative strategy.

The race-dependent power paradigm climaxes in the love triangle that exists among José Darío, María Teresa, and the Mono Espitia. María Teresa is caught in the middle of a deadly "ménage à trois" when her father brokers a marriage with the Mono instead of with José Darío, whom she loves. María Teresa's defiance is a small victory for both women (who typically acquiesce to parental demands) and racial equality. She rejects the upwardly mobile marriage the Mono would provide and, in so doing, repudiates an "unspoken" social practice of

marrying "white" in order to obtain class-based privileges and the better-
ment of the "race." Thus, the implication of "whitening" is foregrounded
in the text when María's decision culminates in violence. Emasculated
by María Teresa's rejection and her love for José Darío, the Mono Espitia resorts to violence to reaffirm his power and manhood. His emasculation by poor, black, disfranchised, and dispossessed rice harvesters
is a social affront that challenges his white privilege and power. Thus, he
compromises María Teresa's marital relationship with José Darío by
raping her. The Mono Espitia thereby reestablishes, in his mind, the social paradigm of white supremacy over the darker dwellers of Los Secos.
The violation of María Teresa and her impregnation recalls the master/
slave relationship of displaced Africans, who were regarded as property.
The arrangement between the Mono Espitia and María Teresa's father
established her as his purchased possession, and underscores the voice-
lessness of women under patriarchal hegemony. This triangular relationship involving gender, race, and class is prevalent not only in *Tierra*,
but also in subsequent works by this Afro-Colombian author.

In order to reveal the historical-cultural mixing and complex social
interaction of the region, Zapata Olivella manipulates relationships and
cultural traditions within the text. An anthropologist by training, Manuel
Zapata Olivella is well acquainted with the importance of the cultural
signifiers that characterize people. Regional folklore in the form of religious celebrations, music, and dance trace the region's history from the
colonial period, through slavery, to the narrative present. Religion, while
not a predominant theme of this work, serves to expand the cultural parameters of the novel and exposes the interfacing of native traditions
and externally imposed religion. Colonial institutionalization in the New
World manifests itself in the continuance of hegemonic rites such as
Saint Bernard's Day and Good Friday:

> The twentieth of August arrived, day of the festivities in honor of Saint
> Bernard and all the townspeople gathered in the church in order to par-
> ticipate in the procession.
>
> (Llegó el 20 de agosto, día de la festividad de San Bernardo, y todo el
> pueblo se reunió en la iglesia para participar en la procesión.) (*Tierra*, 121)

> It was December 24th, and the country folk had come from all of the
> close areas in order to celebrate Good Friday in Lorca, and the crowd of
> people gave rise to the value of the goods [rice].

(Era 24 de diciembre y los campesinos habían llegado de todos los lu-
gares cercanos para festejar la Nochebuena en Lorca, y la afluencia de
personas dio alza momentánea a los productos.) (*Tierra*, 127)

However, the religious dichotomy between inhabitants of the metropolis and those of rural areas of the region is significant. The narrative
voice alludes to an anti-Christian trend in Los Secos via the schoolteacher, Marco Olivares. Olivares travels from San Bernardo to Los
Secos in order to educate the workers of the rice plantation and raise
their social consciousness by challenging the monotheistic beliefs of the
people, and the existence and purpose of God. These "country folk" regard Good Friday as a commercial rather than a religious holiday. It is
a good day for commerce marked by an increase in price of goods sold
on this day of festivity and goodwill. The focus on Good Friday as an
opportunity to exploit consumers minimizes the religious implications
associated with the celebration. The catholic significance of the holiday
is ignored by the protagonists who make no reference to its meaning.
Consequently, Zapata Olivella creates an interpretive space where the
reader is forced to speculate on the sincerity of the people in their ob-
servance of this and other religious observances. The people of Los
Secos exhibit distress at having been forsaken by Christian saints, an attitude developed further in *En Chimá* For those in Los Secos, nature is
the object of their allegiance, worship, and praise. For them, nature is a
godlike force motivating reverence and superstitious rituals:

Nature also was abandoning them. The rains were delayed and summer
was prolonged until very early in the year. This lull was taken advantage
of by the sea, that victoriously floated above the river, carrying its cursed
waters towards the crops; the white coat of the sodium nitrate was a sign
of death and desolation.

(La Naturaleza también los abandonaba. Las lluvias demoraban y el verano se prolongaba hasta muy entrado el año. Esta tregua era apro-
vechada por el mar, que trascendía victorioso sobre el río, llevando sus
aguas malditas hasta los cultivos; la capa blanca de salitre era señal de
muerte y desolación.) (*Tierra*, 240)

Above their heads an owl hurled its ominous hoot and yet, again, in
order to confirm that death was nigh, a tinkling owl loosened his magical
powers from the high point of the heavens.

> (Por encima de sus cabezas un buho lanzó su grito agorero y todavía, una
> vez más, para confirmar de que la muerte se acercaba, una lechuza cas-
> cabelera desgranó su talismo desde lo alto del cielo.) (*Tierra*, 258)

Nature, emblematic of a hostile religious deity, has cursed Los Secos.
The sea and owls become messengers of nature, warning of death and
destruction, similar to the messenger-angels of Christianity. The life-
saving river replaces God the provider. The river is revered as the "savior," the force that sustains existence within the Sinú River valley:

> The river is our salvation . . . it brings to us from afar the fish that we eat;
> it fights on our behalf against the sea in order to stop the salty waters
> from spoiling the rice. We owe everything to the river; that is why the
> teacher calls it Father River.
>
> (El río es la salvación para nosotros ... El nos trae desde muy lejos los
> peces que comemos; lucha contra el mar para impedir que el agua sal-
> ada pudra el arroz. Todo se lo debemos; por eso el maestro lo llama
> Padre Río.) (*Tierra*, 210)

This allegiance to nature reflects the popular belief system of these regional people who have lost hope in the promises and protection of
Catholicism. There is a repositioning and rearticulation of the concepts
of nature and "god." Nature, in all of her manifestations, becomes a
mimetic representation of divinity. The reflection of God in nature is
congruent with African cosmology and offers yet another example of
religious syncretism in *Tierra*. In reference to the projection of nature
within an African tradition, John S. Mbiti observes the following relative to God and nature:

> According to African peoples, man lives in a religious universe, so that
> natural phenomena and objects are intimately associated with God.
> They not only originate from Him but also bear witness to Him. Man's
> understanding of God is strongly coloured by the universe of which man
> is himself a part. Man sees in the universe not only the imprint of but the
> reflection of God.[6]

Textual evidence supports the claim that those of Los Secos view nature as a godlike force that is the provider, sustainer, comforter, and
giver and taker of life.

---

6. John S. Mbiti, *African Religions and Philosophy* (Oxford: Heinemann, 1990), 48.

Other cultural manifestations embedded within the text include a variety of folkloric expressions entrenched in Old World tradition. Oral tradition, folktales, music, and dance become signifiers of an Africanized heritage. Characters such as Carrillito and "el viejo Goyo," Gregorio, embody the spirit of the African griot or Old World storytellers. As in the anancy tales of African tradition, animals become major players in allegorical anecdotes like the "Brer Rabbit" tales. The role of master storyteller is bequeathed to Gregorio as he retells the folktales of the region, principally, "Tío Congrejo" and "Tía Tigra."

Other cultural references with distinguishable African characteristics include *fandango* and *cumbia*. *Fandango* and *cumbia*, today regarded as Afro-Hispanic dance forms, display rhythms and movements that are notably African. Their roots are traced to survival tactics instituted by marooned slaves in Latin America. Both are cultural by-products of the efforts of African slaves to resist assimilation in order to maintain cultural vestiges of the Old World and to subvert New World expressions. *Cumbia* is geographically linked to the locale of *Tierra*. Although understood to reflect rural articulations of Colombia and Panamá, *cumbia* is regarded today as an expression of national Colombian culture. In the narrative, they exemplify the intensity of Manuel Zapata Olivella's focus on historical cultural evolution in a territory branded by miscegenation, racism, ethnic whitening, and cultural syncretism.

A final significant cultural element is language, which emerges as a discernible marker of regional identity. Language has served as a means of resisting cultural hegemony and imperial dominance in many spaces of the African diaspora. Lexicology often fluctuates between the use of the dominant discourse and one colored with regional dialects, which allow for the identification of a people based on speech patterns, diction, and regional connotations of words. In *Tierra*, regional signifiers that connote nonconventional (as determined by the Royal Academy of the Spanish language) meanings allow the dwellers of the Sinú River valley to reclaim their cultural past. "Standard," official language, or the dominant discourse, is subverted into dialectical codes, which can be deciphered only by members of the region. Thus, linguistic signifiers constructed in the Los Secos have meanings that are distinct from those of the "official" discourse. *Caimán*, for example is the officially accepted designation for alligator in the Spanish language. In Los Secos, however, *ronchudo*, the accepted term, is adopted. Likewise, *sarda* is substituted for *tiburón*, or shark. Language variance is so extensive in *Tierra* that the novel includes a glossary of regional terminology.

Tierra allows Manuel Zapata Olivella to reveal many of the complexities of the Sinú River valley region of Colombia. The emphasis on the experiences of Afro-Colombians and the poor set the stage for future narrative development. His ability to write fiction with realistic and naturalist tones places the reader onto the terrain and into the reality of the Sinú River valley dwellers. Cultural syncretism based in historical miscegenation is explored as characters and relationships engender competing ideologies of culture and racial/ethnic identification. Regional language adds uniqueness to the geographical adaptation of Zapata Olivella's novel and further validates the novel as an example of a Colombian regional text. Moreover, the text recovers from the margins the regional black experience. People of African descent are the primary protagonists, and they do not function as representations of socially contrived stereotypes. The emphasis here is on the Afro-Colombian experience, a counternarration of black reality in Latin American, one opposed to that of many mainstream writers in Latin America. Social realism surfaces as a major thematic trope in the works of Zapata Olivella, as he chronicles the exploitation, oppression, poverty, and societal abuse of Afro-Colombians. The thematic shift in character portrayal delineates a major shift in the course of national and regional literary representation and distinguishes Zapata Olivella's work from that of his literary contemporaries. *Tierra* commences this author's practice of literary "darkening," an essentialist characteristic of his literary aesthetic.

Chapter II

From Region to Nation to North America

Manuel Zapata Olivella's first published work revealed his desire to insert social polemics within the confined geographical spaces of his narrative. The narrative focus on a district (the Sinú River valley) in his first novel continues in later works. With *Tierra*, Zapata Olivella was well on his way toward establishing himself among his literary contemporaries. In an effort to "globalize" his readership, Olivella complexified the textual interplay among people, locations, and public spheres. Geographies are of utmost importance and emerge as an advancing literary aesthetic in subsequent works of the Afro-Colombian writer. From *Tierra, Pasión, He visto, China,* and *En Chimá,* to *Changó,* to name but a few, locality and the sociopolitical maneuvering of inhabitants drive the narrative discourse and become dominant protagonists in and of themselves. With *He visto,* Chicago, New York, Los Angeles, and other North American localities are personified within the text and emerge as tangible beings that live and breathe. As the reader engages with the text, the public spheres presented tangle with the characters within, creating a stylistic symbiosis of land mass and inhabitants.

Two years after writing *Tierra,* Zapata Olivella produced two seminal works, *Pasión* and *He visto.* Probably conceived as one complete work, these two texts are complementary and serve as the genesis for Zapata Olivella's discourse on the Americas. Although *He visto* was written in 1949, it was not published until 1953. In both works, the stark textual geographical shift from Central America to Mexico and northward distinguishes the works, while many of Zapata Olivella's most salient themes, such as poverty, hunger, and discrimination, remain the same. Thus, the thematic consistency allows the writer to cross temporal and geographical boundaries while intensifying his critique of human interactions and experiences.

An important characteristic of Zapata Olivella is multigenre writing. Regarded as autobiographical by certain scholars (Jackson and others) of Afro-Hispanic literature, these next works represent a literary shift from prose fiction to quasi-autobiography. Although Jackson and others' assertions are understandable, given the similarity between the author's life and the accounts related in both works, additional scholarship and clarification are needed. As Richard Jackson observes:

> In Latin America, however, the black autobiography is not a primary form, although autobiographical books by Afro-Latin Americans do exist, including Candelario Obeso's *La lucha de la vida* (1882), Manuel Zapata Olivella's *Pasión vagabunda* (1949) and his *He visto la noche* (1959) in Colombia, Martín Morúa Delgado's *La familia Unzúazu* (1901), and *Biografía de un cimarrón* (1966) in Cuba.[1]

I am not convinced, however, that this highly gifted and precociously maturing young man and writer was experimenting with the autobiographical novel here.

Although this chapter will focus principally on *He visto*, *Pasión* definitely merits some analysis. Within these two works, the reader witnesses the intellectual growth of young Manuel as his views are challenged through interactions in locations throughout his travels. Thus, in addition to learning about the social lives of others, the narrator discovers much about himself. Through the "fictional" chronicling of the journeys, the author's true passions are revealed regarding books, people, geographies, and travel.

In both *Pasión* and *He visto* the basic premise is straightforward. Both document the adventures of a young man as he moves from regions to nations in search of an amplified perspective on life. The Colombian Ministry of Culture commissioned a 2000 edition of both novels in one volume in recognition of Zapata Olivella's literary accomplishments. This distinction attests to the author's status as a major contributor to Colombian letters. *Pasión* is recognized in particular as a fine literary achievement. Noted Colombian literary figure Germán Espinosa offers the following summation of *Pasión:*

> *Pasión vagabunda*, in a concise and eloquent prose relates a series of compulsive trips that the author undertook without a cent in his pocket and being such, without means to pay for himself along the way, joyful or dreadfully on foot.

---

1. Richard L. Jackson, *Black Writers in Latin America* (Albuquerque: University of New Mexico Press, 1979), 28.

(*Pasión vagabunda*, en una prosa escueta y desenvuelta, relata una serie de viajes compulsivos, que el autor emprendió sin un centavo en su bolsillo y, por tanto, sin con qué costearse en vehículo, alborozada o atrozmente a pie.) (*Pasión*, XV)

Scholars such as Marvin Lewis and Richard Jackson corroborate Espinosa's impressions. In essence, *Pasión* charts Zapata Olivella's narrative trek from South America, through Central America, and into Mexico. The protagonist leaves Bogotá poor in terms of finances but wealthy in terms of ambition as he embarks upon a series of adventures in search of a heightened understanding of "self," the world, and humanity. This text, then, represents a much larger, multidimensional puzzle piece than his earlier work. In *Pasión*, the protagonist is obliged to negotiate landspace, comprehend new social attitudes, discover history, and confront new cultures, all by way of human interaction.

Manuel Zapata Olivella's *He visto*, his third published piece, can be viewed as a sequel to the work that preceded it, *Pasión*. It too is a "travelogue" that traces the journey of the protagonist from Colombia to the United States, much like the author Manuel Zapata Olivella himself, who had just suspended his studies, and with very little financial support, embarked upon a sojourn that would alter his life by challenging his worldview and enriching his literary career. Like *Pasión*, this work has few scholarly assessments, which might cause readers to underestimate the importance of this relatively short text. A surface read would cause one to conclude that the piece is a "diary" of sorts that relates incidents in the life of a vagabond wanderer, presumably the author himself, as he travels from Mexico to the United States. However, tucked between the lines is an important discourse on race and the United States that is quite compelling. Laurence Prescott's "Afro-Northamérica en los escritos de viaje de Manuel Zapata Olivella: Hacia los orígenes de *He visto la noche*" is the sole scholarly article devoted to this text. Although Prescott's article is not a literary critique of the work per se, it does situate it in light of his other pieces, primarily essays, offering a propagandistic critique of the United States. In his concluding paragraph, Prescott asserts that forgotten or lost essays such as "Miserias de Nueva York: Harlem olvidado" (New York miseries: Harlem forgotten) are of great significance in understanding the etiological development of *He visto*:

Finally, the study of these articles offer us clues that facilitate a more profound understanding of the creative and organizational process that gave birth to *He visto la noche* and, probably to other works whose roots lie buried in unknown or forgotten texts of Zapata Olivella that have yet to be rediscovered.

(Por último, el estudio de estos artículos nos ofrece claves que permiten un conocimiento más profundo del proceso creativo y organizador que dio origen a *He visto la noche* y, probablemente, a otras obras cuyas raíces yacen enterradas en textos desconocidos u olvidados de Zapata Olivella que todavía quedan por redescubrir.) (*He visto*, 58)

Prescott suggests that the literary precursors to *He visto*'s exposition are the essays Zapata Olivella wrote prior to the publication of the text. Additionally, Prescott makes an aesthetic connection between the author's early works and subsequent ones through the thematic focus on blackness. Finally, it is noteworthy that Prescott's essay is a revised and lengthened version of his prologue to the 2000 edition of the text. Hopefully, this signifies an increased readership for the text, translating into more scholarship on this and other works.

Published in 1953 by Editorial Los Andes in Bogotá, *He visto* serves as a transitional text between the 1940s and the 1950s. Richard Jackson describes the piece as "a little book he wrote in 1946 and first published in 1953."[2] Zapata Olivella's literary aesthetic to this point centers on the survival of the downtrodden, a focus that becomes critical to his writerly and humanistic development. The development in his literary trajectory is fourfold. First, in *Tierra, Pasión,* and *He visto,* the author's personal growth constitutes the vantage point. In his first work, he focuses on the complexities of his home region and ecological challenges of the Sinú River valley. *Pasión* reflects Zapata Olivella's thirst for exploration and his desire to broaden his knowledge of the Americas as he journeys from Colombia through Central America and seeks refuge in Mexico. *He visto* is the continuation of this exploratory trek as the author depicts the challenges and confrontations in a "modernized" United States. Second, these three texts represent a movement from "home" into the "world" as the author's focus shifts from regional, to national, to international concerns. Third, each text presents a different focus on race relations and racism, allowing one to chart the development of this author's focus on the oppressed and dispossessed as it comes full circle in his latter works. Finally, the pervasive theme of

2. Ibid., 90.

poverty surfaces in all his works. *Tierra* deals with the systemic manifestations of poverty in rural settings, the rice plantations of the Sinú River valley. The rural poor are his focus in Central America and Mexico in *Pasión*. However, with *He visto* bucolic representations of poverty yield to scenes of urban poverty, primarily in Los Angeles, Chicago, and Harlem.

He visto encompasses forty-five short pieces or "chapters." These chapters offer recollections of people, places, and events that were most memorable on the protagonist's journey to the United States. The first-person narrator recounts the adventures of a vagabond traveler who follows a meandering route through the United States. Because the accounts reflect the writer's past experiences, Richard Jackson and Laurence Prescott argue that this work represents the author's life following his leave of absence from the university. Jackson further states that the entries in *He visto* can best be described as a compilation of "travelogues." Consequently, the line of demarcation between fiction and reality is blurred in this text as it is in *Pasión*. Additionally, there is a *trabalenguas*, or tongue twister, that further meshes fiction and reality. In Los Angeles, a woman from his past recognizes the narrator/protagonist. The undeveloped female character cries out: "You are Manuel Bapata, Zapata, Olivella, Oliviera!" (¡Usted es Manuel Bapata, Zapata, Olivella, Oliveira! *He visto*, 286), but the narrative voice does not succinctly confirm his identity. He merely responds affirmatively to an identity that affords him anonymity. And, in this anonymity, the play between fiction and reality is apparent. There are no other distinct references to the first-person narrator, leaving the reader to assume that the pronominal reference is to Manuel Zapata Olivella and not the distorted construction rendered in the text. As the unidentified female character tries to pinpoint an identity using parts of the author's identity, the reader is lulled into making a direct association or connection between the author and narrator.

In addition to the fictional/reality blurring, an aesthetic of stylistic borrowing is in existence. The literary style of *He visto* can be compared to that of *Lazarillo de Tormes*, a classical example of the Spanish picaresque novel. *He visto* charts the adventures and pilgrimage of the protagonist in the style of the picaresque. These adventures expose the reader to new environments, the inhabitants that occupy them, and the characters with whom the protagonist interacts. The protagonist in *He visto*, like that in *Lazarillo*, is a first-person, omniscient narrator that recounts his countless adventures from numerous geographical spaces. From encounters, experiences, and observations, the protagonist's sense of consciousness is raised and his worldview is expanded. Major themes in the text are U.S. imperialism, race, racism, and black hunger (a term that will be explained later in the chapter). In addition, linear chronology is revealed through historical references. The initial paragraph mentions the testing of the atomic bomb in Hiroshima and Nagasaki, a reference that indicates the decade involved and further globalizes the text.

It will be remembered that *He visto* is the author's second text written during his hiatus from his medical studies at the University of Bogotá. *Pasión* records the meandering of the protagonist from Colombia culminating with his illegal entry into Mexico and his days as a journalist for the most prestigious Mexican journal of the time, *Tiempo.* The conclusion of *Pasión* becomes the point of departure for Olivella's third published work, *He visto.* Narratively, the author connects the texts in the first chapter of the work, "Una visa para EE.UU." (A visa for the U.S.):

> When I got out of the taxi at the Mexican railway station, it was already too late to take the train that transported the Mexican journalists invited by the United States government to witness the testing of the atomic bomb at Bikini Reef. So, my hustle and bustle of many days trying to incorporate myself on that trip representing a Mexican magazine ended. The smoking funnel of the engine that I could see in the distance shook the pretexts of my old vagabond passion.
>
> (Cuando salté del taxi en la estación de los ferrocarriles de México ya era demasiado tarde para tomar el tren que conducía a los periodistas mexicanos invitados por el gobierno de los Estados Unidos a presenciar la prueba de la bomba atómica en el atolón de Bikini. Así terminaban mis ajetreos de varios días por incorporarme a ese viaje en representación de una revista mexicana. La chimenea humeante de la locomotora que alcancé a ver en la distancia conmovió las asideros de mi vieja pasión vagabunda.) (*He visto,* 241)

He visto can best be described as a sociological exploration from Mexico to an inner-city dwelling of the United States. The narrative voice corroborates this shift by stating at the end of the first paragraph that humankind is the object of "discovery" in the travels of the protagonist: "A new concept about life blossomed in my globetrotter mind as a result of the contact with the aggressive Mexican town. If before the routes and the landscape moved my restless feet, now mankind has become the object of my discovery." (Un nuevo concepto de la vida florecía en mi mente de trotamundos al contacto del combativo pueblo mexicano. Si antes las rutas y el paisaje movían a inquietud mis pasos, ahora el hombre se convertía en el objeto de mi descubrimiento. *He visto*, 241) As the citation indicated, the protagonist's motivation has changed. The journey is no longer a topographical discovery but one focused on humankind and the negotiation of environment.

It is generally accepted by scholars that human ecology as an academic discipline is a branch of sociology that explores the relationship between the human community and its environment and the spatial and temporal interrelationship between economic, social and political enterprise. In *He visto*, Zapata Olivella uses human ecology to present a skillfully orchestrated "exposé" of the United States, the place where black Americans interface with the social, political, and economic forces of the majority culture.

Using the construct of human ecology as a theoretical paradigm for analysis, we can explore Olivella's views on race in the urban United States. Much in the manner of the Spanish picaresque novel, the narrator pilgrimages through the United States where racial conflicts are everywhere. During these sojourns, the narrator encounters hunger, poverty, racism, and discrimination, which serve to awaken his race consciousness.

Structurally, the text can best be described as a narrative journal in that each "chapter" reads as if it were an entry based on the interaction of the protagonist with a specific environment. The forty-five chapters that chronicle the protagonist's travels are laced with subjective and objective observations on race. Richard Jackson states: "Racism and discrimination in the United States have been persistent concerns in black Latin American literature, concerns which, together with United States imperialism have, indeed, pervaded much of Latin American literature in general."[3] Numerous works by late-nineteenth- and twentieth-century Latin American literary figures from Cuba's José Martí to Colombia's Manuel Zapata Olivella bear out Jackson's observation. The Latin American preoccupation with imperialism is the direct result of other countries' oppressive late-nineteenth- and early-twentieth-century foreign policy toward Latin America. One event that shaped Latin American

3. Ibid., 144.

hostility was the Spanish American War of 1898. A war that should have involved Spain and Cuba led to U.S. intervention and concluded with the United States actually controlling Puerto Rico, Guam, and Cuba. The Treaty of Paris, which concluded the war, was viewed as a document sanctioning imperialism and hegemony in the New World. Additionally, the dawn of the twentieth century witnessed the United States's intervention in Latin America relative to what is now the Republic of Panama. Panama had been a province of Colombia, but in 1903 the people of Panama rose in revolt and declared independence. In 1911, fearing that the Panama Canal might fall under foreign control, U.S. bankers gained control of the National Bank of Nicaragua and the government-owned railway. In 1917, the United States purchased the Virgin Islands, fearing that the Germans might use the islands as a naval base in the Caribbean. During the rise of fascism and the onset of World War II, the United States sought to promote solidarity in the Western hemisphere by sponsoring conferences in Uruguay, Argentina, and Peru between 1933 and 1938. Thus, the history of late-nineteenth- and early-twentieth-century Latin America and the United States is plagued with problematic and oppositional policies, an understanding of which facilitates a better understanding of Zapata Olivella's critique in this text.

For black Latin Americans however, hostility toward U.S. foreign policy was linked to their belief that white America was inherently racist. Many black Latin Americans feared that U.S. intervention would lead to increased oppression and subjugation as a result of "double-other": black and Latin American. Fully cognizant of the (mis)treatment and disfranchisement of blacks in a Jim Crow America, black Latin Americans could justify their fear of U.S. imperialism. The racial climate in the United States during the time frame of *He visto* was tumultuous. Marred by incidents of lynching, the documented reality of second-class citizenry, and involuntary displacement, life for black Americans continued to remind a hypocritical United States that the democracy and equal rights it preached abroad were elusive goals on home soil. Hence, the history of the United States during the first half of the twentieth century engendered much suspicion on the part of Latin Americans in general, and black Latin Americans in particular.

One of the earliest human ecological episodes in the novel involves the history of migrant workers that fled to the United States after World War II in search of work. Primarily unskilled laborers, many ventured to northern industries and southern crop-producing territories. The narrator in the first chapter "Una visa para EE.UU." informs the reader of how he was able to leave Mexico and head for the border of the United States. The casualties of the war and the economic deterioration that followed created a need for a cheap labor supply throughout the United States, but especially to work in fruit groves and produce fields in southern states. Allusions are made to farmers from Texas coming to Mexico and in some cases taking Mexicans illegally to their farms and groves. By "hitching" a ride on one of the illegal transports, the protagonist intends to enter the United States after having failed on a prior attempt:

> Many days later, another opportunity to head Northward presented itself to me, if I were lucky. . . . North American farmers that did not get ready for the thousand of workers decimated by the war, urgently needed rural Mexicans to harvest their next maturing crops on the large plantations of the South.

> (Varios días después se me presentó otra oportunidad de partir al norte, si la suerte me acompañaba ... Los agricultores norteamericanos que no disponían de los miles de obreros diezmados por la guerra, estaban urgidos de campesinos mexicanos para recoger sus cosechas próximas a madurar en las grandes plantaciones del Sur.) (*He visto*, 242)

As the protagonist and other Mexican workers prepare to cross into Texas, the social and economic conditions of Mexican border towns come clearly into focus. This description is detailed further in the chapter "Exodo" (Exodus). Here, the protagonist recounts the inhumane treatment of the Mexican workers and depicts their fear of the "Americans." The physical examination is meticulously described: nude in the basement of a building, the workers are examined by medical doctors who order them to open their mouths, spit, bend over and not be assholes: (¡Abrir boca! ¡Puje! ¡Agacha! ¡No ser bruto! *He visto*, 248) However, the most troubling incident that reveals how the Yankees view the Mexicans occurs in the chapter entitled "Granado humano" (Human cattle). Reminiscent of the treatment of slaves during the transatlantic holocaust, the cleansing process of those crossing from Mexico to North America degrades the exploited workers:

> After having repeated many times that their clothing should be placed on the small bench in front of them, they were ordered to strip nude. Soon afterwards, half a dozen men appeared each with sprayers of DDT, and turning them on, they covered the group in a cloud of insecticide.

The unexpected bath awakened general hilarity: men, clothing, shoes and sandals were impregnated with the deadly powder.

(Después de indicar repetidas veces que las ropas debían ponerse en la banqueta frente a ellos, se dio la orden de desnudarse. Muy pronto media docena de hombres aparecieron con sendos atomizadores de D.D.T., y haciéndolos funcionar, envolvieron la batallón en una nube de insecticida. El baño imprevisto despertó la hilaridad general: hombres, ropas, zapatos y huaraches quedaron impregnados del mortífero polvo.) (*He visto*, 252)

The act of disinfecting Mexicans is similar to the delousing or debugging of cattle. As if they were infected with pathogens and parasites that would "contaminate" the purity of the citizens of the United States, the Mexicans were bathed in dichlorodiphenyltrichloronane, colloquially referred to as DDT. These passages reveal America's imperialist attitude toward its closest southern neighbor. The language evokes images recalling the dehumanizing institution of slavery. The text reveals the 1940s in the United States as a time of white social, political, and economic dominance. Black Americans and other ethnic minorities were regarded as second-class citizens in a land that was supposed to grant freedom, liberty, and justice to all who sought refuge there. Thus, the act of bathing and disinfecting the Mexican migrant workers can be interpreted symbolically as an act of purification for entrance into America, as if their "uncleanness" would contaminate in some way the social fabric of the United States.

Before beginning "Granado humano," the third chapter, the narrator prepares the reader for the magnitude of Mexicans that were soon to be displaced in the United States: "We had not gotten off when another train filled with hundreds of workers continued towards the north. I realized that that same day two more trains had departed packed with countrymen and then I understood the magnitude of the exodus. Mexico was losing blood." (No habíamos bajado, cuando otro tren cargado de cientos de braceros seguía para el norte. Me informé que aquel mismo día habían partido dos trenes más abarrotados de campesinos y entonces comprendí la magnitud del éxodo. México se desangraba. *He visto*, 250). Conscious of the extremity of the situation regarding the migration of impoverished Mexicans searching for opportunities in the United States, the protagonist is taken aback by the implications of the reality. In the concluding sentence, Mexico is personified as someone slowly bleeding to death. This transitions perfectly as "blood" also becomes a signifier of the loss of identity and cultural ethnicity. Thus, as the narrative shifts into the third chapter, the themes of imperialism, miscegenation, and assimilation of Mexicans converge in the character of the chief hiring authority: "I began speaking with the chief of hiring, a North American of Aztec blood who was proud of his Mexican origin in order to win over the sympathy of the workers, but who had a mentality one-hundred percent Yankee." (Me puse al habla con el jefe de la contratación, un norteamericano de sangre azteca que se preciaba de su origen mexicano para ganarse la simpatía de los braceros, pero que tenía una mentalidad ciento por ciento yanqui. *He visto*, 250). The double-identity/ethnic construction transforms into an appropriated mental attitude that is described as wholly North American. The reader can infer that this character of mixed heritage has been assimilated wholly into the dominant cultural ideology of the United States. This introduces an assimilationist discourse into the text. A palimpsest of identities converges into one hegemonic nature wherein Western thought dominates body and identity politics.

As the protagonist moves north, the urban situations allow his voice to exploit one particular component of Hispanic representation: black Hispanics. The narrator emphasizes the "corporality" of black Hispanics as they navigate their new geographical space. He exaggerates the impression black Hispanics have on their tangible environment. The focus then is on the indelible impact the "Africanized" being has on the white mainstream. Black Hispanics are seen as fetishized and eroticized:

> One of the things that fascinated them was the psychology of the Black Latino, since it contrasted openly with that of the North American. The possibilities of educating themselves, fraternizing with those of other races, their roots still in the most haughty of families—at least in some countries—and its few racial prejudices afforded a different mentality to the Black Hispanic American. Also, they cared for our folklore, but not in the function of its form, but of its liveliness. On more than one occasion, Ruth, who had learned from Maudel black dance rhythms, began to imitate my movements when she tried to dance the Colombian *cumbia* or the *porro* while Jorge, silent, barely illuminated by the brilliance of the record player observed our confused bodies engrossed in the shades of the night brawn against the walls of the room.
>
> (Una de las cosas que más les encantaba era la psicología del negro latino, pues contrastaba abriertamente con la del norteamericano. Sus

posibilidades para educarse, de fraternizar con los de otras razas, su raigambre aun en las más encopetada familias—al menos en algunos paises—y sus pocos prejuicios raciales daban una mentalidad distinta al negro hispanoamericano. También les atraía nuestro folklor, pero no en función de su forma, sino de su vivencia. En más de una ocasión, Ruth que había aprendido de Maudel el ritmo negro de la danza, se ponía a imitar mis gestos cuando trataba de bailar la cumbia o el porro colombianos en tanto Jorge, silencioso, apenas alumbrado por el resplandor del tocadiscos, observaba absorto nuestros cuerpos confundidos en las sombras que la noche dibujaba en las paredes del aposento.) (*He visto*, 279)

The citation above attests to the devaluation of human subjects not conforming to culturally configured behaviors that are alien to them. The manner by which those marginalized adapt articulates a strategy of cultural resistance as the black Hispanics impart the corporal and musical rhythms of home to the foreign culture. As these "alien" cultural manifestations confront the dominant signifiers, an ethnocultural integration emerges.

Throughout, the Afro-Latin American is observed and reconstructed by the dominant white culture. Again, it is important to remember that the text covers a period from the mid-1940s to the early 1950s. The history of race relations between blacks and whites in the United States was shaped by postslavery hostility as whites fought vehemently to maintain historical privilege through an oppressive social order supported by Jim Crow ideology. The perception and treatment of blacks by American and Euro-American whites is given center stage in the chapter "Mi vida con Jorge" (My life with Jorge). The narrative presents Jorge, a friend of the protagonist who lives in an all-white, gated community in Los Angeles. The narrator reveals that Jorge helped the protagonist understand the North American way of life "Jorge was the friend that helped me understand the American way of life." (Jorge fue el amigo que me ayudó a entender el sentido de la vida norteamericana. *He visto*, 274) The second sentence of the chapter charts the lineage and ethnocultural composition of Jorge. He is described as being of German parents, born in England and nationalized in the United States after World War I. The geographical depiction of the parents allows one to conclude that he is definitely Anglo-Saxon. However, it is from Jorge that the protagonist learns the meaning of "otherness:"

Already in his experiences and observations, he had entered into the dying resuscitation of the Black North American confused in a civilization that discriminated against him; he spied on the silent battle of the dispossessed Chinese without human rights; he saw the brutal oppression of the Mexican Indian growing before the dashing of the conquerer cowboy and until the arrogant and pedantic Japanese pride preserving their tradition in the midst of iconoclastic North American civilization.

(Ya en sus experiencias y observaciones había penetrado en el agónico resucitar del negro norteamericano confundido en una civilización que lo discriminaba; espió la sorda batalla del chino desterrado y sin derechos humanos; vio la brutal opresión del indio mexicano cediendo ante el embate del *cow-boy* conquistador y hasta el altivo y pedante orgullo japonés salvando su tradición frente a la iconoclasta civilización norteamericana.) (*He visto*, 274)

Because of his association with Jorge and his milieu, the protagonist learns how to navigate this "white" geographical space. Jorge instructs him on how to behave and how to occupy the shared physical space. Jorge invites the protagonist to live with him, where he would feel "at home": "Come live with me. In my house you will be like in that of your parents." (Vente a vivir conmigo. En mi casa estarás como en la de tus padres. *He visto*, 275). Clearly, Jorge's gated community has nothing in common with the protagonist's home in Colombia. Moreover, Jorge's extended hospitality comes with constraints. Jorge instructs the protagonist on how he should interact with the white residents. In the midst of fraternal cordiality, Jorge "flips the script" and reveals the racist ideologies of his community that he partially shares. Jorge instructs the protagonist on how to answer questions about his presence in that neighborhood or with Jorge: "if anyone were to ask you what you are doing here, tell them that you are my servant" (pero si alguien te preguntara qué haces en ella, responde que eres mi sirviente, *He visto*, 275). The discrimination intensifies when Jorge explains to his Latin American "friend" that in this all-white neighborhood, blacks are only allowed as servants. The words of Jorge are validated when the protagonist interacts with the neighbors:

His brusque words resonated in my ears a while, but days later I understood it all when an elderly woman, ridiculously dressed and who spent the day tormenting us from the vicinity rehearsing unsuccessfully all types of arias, asked me: What are you doing in 7125 West? She was referring to the number of Jorge's house. I am his mechanical helper. I responded without being able to let the word servant gust out of me. My explanation satisfied the old blonde, then she left with her nose curled up in the air as if she had smelled Satan. When I told Jorge what had happened, he said to me: If you had not told her that you were my servant, within a few hours they would have demanded that I move to the Black neighborhood with you.

(Sus palabras sonaron en mis oídos un tanto bruscas, pero días más tarde lo comprendí todo cuando una señora de edad, adefeciosamente vestida y que se pasaba el día atormentándonos desde la vencindad ensayando sin éxito toda clase de arias, me preguntó: ¿Qué hace usted en el 7125 West? —Se refiere al número de la casa de Jorge. —Soy su ayudante de mecánica. —Respondí sin que me hubiera podido brotar la palabra *sirviente*. Satisfizo mi explicación al rubio vejestorio, pues se marchó con su nariz espingada como si hubiera olfateado a Satanás. Cuando le conté a Jorge lo sucedido, me dijo: —Si no hubieras dicho que estabas a mi servicio, dentro de pocas horas me habrán exigido que me mudara contigo al barrio de los negros.) (*He visto*, 275)

This exchange is significant for three reasons. First, the reader is made aware of the social discriminatory and racist ideology of the post–World War II United States. Racial segregation is the order of the day as blacks almost everywhere are marginalized and segregated. Second, it illustrates that racism is a cultural phenomenon that prescribes behavior for whites and blacks. Because having a black Latino servant poses no immediate threat to the status quo, Jorge feels secure in his suggestion. Although his "friend" is a double "other," being both Latino and of African descent, his "Latinoness" is effaced wholly by his blackness. Finally, race here is defined by phenotypic characteristics. Because the Hispanic protagonist was not visibly "white," he was treated as black. "Otherness" is defined by color, not geography. Although Jorge was not born in the United States, his European ancestry and his phenotypic composition allow him to integrate and assimilate into "whiteness," a luxury not afforded his friend. Identity is imposed from "without," not from "within." Regardless of the identity assumed by the protagonist, it is negotiated in the public sphere by whites that define him by semiotic markers prescribed for blackness. This experience confuses the protagonist, who believes the United States to be the land of the free, home of equality. The protagonist learns that freedom extends only to whites. For blacks, America is the home of hunger, poverty, racism, and discrimination, especially in Chicago and Harlem, New York.

Textually, the protagonist experienced Jim Crow ideology long before his arrival in Chicago and New York. As revealed in the text, he encountered American racism in Texas, Utah, and California. Those incidents prepared him for what was to come. In Chicago, bags in hand, the narrator sets out in search of affordable accommodations. He finds a cheap hotel inhabited principally by Spanish-speaking persons. However, the protagonist is chagrined to learn that the owner, a Panamanian woman, and tenants do not welcome him as a fellow South American. In fact, these Hispanic transplants have (re)negotiated their ethnicity:

> In a poverty-stricken building, from where a small bulletin board hung, I deduced that I could find cheap housing. With great surprise, I found out that the owner was a Panamanian woman and that the hotel was overpopulated with Latinos. For a minute I hoped to meet friendly faces and expressions among them, but those beings had already lost their Hispanicity. They only spoke English and felt no curiosity about a recently arrived Spanish-speaker. The germ of mechanization and that of big cities had dehumanized them.
>
> (En un edificio de pobrísmo aspecto, de donde colgaba la tablilla de un hotel, deduje que podía encontrar alojamiento barato. Con gran sorpresa me enteré que la propietaria era una panameña y que el establecimiento estaba superpoblado de latinos. Por un instante creí encontrar expresiones y rostros amigos entre ellos, pero ya estos seres habían perdido su hispanidad. Hablaban sólo el inglés y no sentían ninguna curiosidad por un recién llegado de habla española. El germen del maquinismo y de las granded ciudades los habían deshumanizado.) (*He visto*, 299)

The fact that both the Panamanian hotel owner and the others were indifferent to the arrival of a Spanish-speaking guest was perplexing to the protagonist. In order to rationalize their behavior, he concludes that they have been "dehumanized," infected by the harmful bacteria of their exiled environment: the cold, impersonal streets of a large urban metropolis. Perhaps the Hispanics chose to rid themselves of all traces of Hispanicity in order to blend better into the mainstream, thereby attempting to escape oppression and discrimination. Such an observation would conform to the practice of why many non-Americans sought to elude the discrimination and prejudice directed toward them. For blacks denied the opportunity to renegotiate their ethnicity, there is only poverty, hunger, and hopelessness. All are pandemic in black communities.

The next chapter, "El Chicago Negro," depicts black resistance in

Chicago during the late 1940s. Largely due to the promulgation of black nationalist ideology through print media, religion, and other institutionalized elements within the black community, the narrator views Chicago as the Mecca for black resistance: "Chicago is the spirit of Black resistance. From there, magazines, books, pamphlets, and programs that sustain the great struggle against negrophobia in Chicago itself, in New York, in Washington and the discriminating bastions of the South emerge." (Chicago es el espíritu de la resistencia negra. De allí salen los magazines, libros, folletos y programas que sustentan la gran lucha contra la negrofobia en el mismo Chicago, en Nueva York, en Washington y el los bastiones discriminatorios del Sur. *He visto,* 308) The Chicago experiences of the protagonist culminate in his joining the black struggle and resistance. Witnessing many forms of social protest while in Chicago and in other locales inspires the protagonist to write articles exposing the plight of those of African ancestry in Latin America. In his writings, the narrator advocates cooperative dialogue in order to combat continental white supremacy. He underscores the importance of print media in promoting the black agenda and heightening consciousness, and he lauds the national importance and circulation of the *Chicago Defender.*

The black American religious experience also leaves an indelible mark upon the protagonist. Religion offers a means of resistance and a path to solidarity for the black community. Admitting his intrigue with the New World manifestations of African religions, the narrator centers the manner in which urban blacks in the United States have constructed a religious expression that suits their cultural heritage. The protagonist witnesses religious fanaticism during a baptism conducted by Father Divine, a black, godlike evangelist, reminiscent of the Oricha Changó and a black "savior." In the midst of oppression in Chicago's Black Belt, religion emerges as an inherently black phenomenon. Intrigued by the African expressions found in the black worship experience, the protagonist undergoes a catharsis when he compares North American practices with those with which he is familiar:

> Religious practices of Black people awakened my interest and a profound emotional reaction. I was always concerned with the African origins of the traditions in my country, and influenced by the teachings of the Brazilian Africanist Nina Rodríguez, I looked for the similarity that religious practices of Black North Americans could have with those of Latinos, both being tributaries of Africa.

(Las prácticas religiosas de los negros despertaban mi interés y una profunda reacción emocional. Siempre me inquietaron las fuentes africanas de las tradiciones en mi país, e influido por las lecturas del africanista brasileño, Nina Rodríguez, busqué la similitud que pudiera tener las prácticas religiosas de los negros norteamericanos con las de los latinos, por ser ambas tributarias del Africa.) (*He visto*, 312)

From the rite of baptism to the possession by spirits, vestiges of Old World religiosity are interwoven into the New World religious practices of the sons and daughters of Africa.

The final geographical space analyzed under the sociological paradigm of human ecology is artistic expression in Harlem. The postwar and postdepression socioeconomic conditions oblige many impoverished blacks to stay at Mill's Hotel, the only place they, and the protagonist, can afford. In New York, the deplorable conditions resulting from poverty, overcrowding, homelessness, hopelessness, and despair begin on the stairs of New York's Penn Station subway stop, in the Greyhound bus terminal, or on the benches of Central Park. Disenchanted with life in New York, the protagonist reassesses idealized visions of Harlem in light of the sickening reality:

The Harlem that was in my view was not the marvelous neighborhood that the newspapers talked about. I uselessly searched the street corners for young black boys dancing the swing or women displaying their expensive leather overcoats. Gone were the times when Duke Ellington attracted the white elite to the dancing halls of the Cotton Club, when Louis Armstrong made his golden trumpet sing before the overwhelmed tycoons from lower Manhattan, who only waited until nightfall to appear in the aristocratic salons of Harlem.

(El Harlem que tenía a mi vista no era el barrio maravilloso de que hablaban los periódicos. Inútilmente buscaba en las esquinas a los negritos bailando el *swing* y a las mujeres luciendo costosísimos abrigos de pieles. Muy atrás estaban los tiempos cuando Duke Ellington atraía la élite blanca a los salones del Cotton Club, cuando Louis Armstrong vocalizaba su trompeta de oro frente a los atónitos magnates de la ciudad baja de Nueva York, quienes sólo esperaban la caída de la noche para aparecer en los salones aristocráticos de Harlem.) (*He visto*, 360)

Present-day Harlem overflows with society's dispossessed and rejected, many of whom are descendants of migrants who arrived at Ellis Island with high hopes for a better life. These downtrodden (ranging from former war veterans and oppressed blacks to refugees from foreign nations) represent the current reality of a space that purportedly "flowed with milk and honey." For those depicted in the text, neither opportunities nor milk and honey were easily found. As the narrator navigates Harlem and interfaces with the "hunger" of numerous immigrants from France, Germany, Haiti, and the Caribbean Islands and with Americans from across the United States, the narrator's consciousness as well as a desire to fight are awakened. The epiphanic call to action takes the form of literary protest, which is a major characteristic of Zapata Olivella's later works.

In New York, the narrator makes reference to historical events. The opera diva Marian Anderson's performance at Carnegie Hall is mentioned: "During the afternoon of that same day, wandering through the streets of the city, on a corner I discovered a poster announcing for that night a concert of Marian Anderson at Carnegie Hall." (En la tarde de ese mismo día, vagando por las calles de la ciudad, en una esquina describrí un cartel donde se anunciaba para esa noche un concierto de Marian Anderson en el Carnegie Hall. *He visto*, 368). This reference serves to establish historical chronology and to recall the mobilization of blacks. Anderson's denial at Constitution Hall in Washington, D.C., serves as a reminder of discrimination, separatism, protest, struggle, and victory. For the protagonist, Anderson's voice is a hymn of rebellion (un himno de rebelión) against racism in the United States, the oppression of the poor, the multifaceted manifestations of North American hunger and its obsession with excluding "Others."

In New York, the protagonist has a second encounter with the divine father, symbol of black North American religious nationalism. Father Divine inspires hope and offers refuge from the diverse articulations of black American hunger. It is destitute poverty and hunger that bring the protagonist and Father Divine together. In search of a cheap repast, he learns that complete meals can be had at the temple's restaurant. Upon satisfying his physical hunger, he begins to "hunger" for more information about this "Dios Negro" but is given only a mythologized account of Father Divine's omnipresence: "The Father's presence is everywhere. Here in the food, there in the music, in wherever his unlimited goodness is manifested." (La presencia del Padre está en todas partes. Aquí en la comida, allá en la música, en dondequiera que se manifieste su ilimitada bondad. *He visto*, 335) For the blacks who believe, the temple and sanctuary of Father Divine ensure a space where one can escape the social ills of racial discrimination and white supremacy. For those who do not believe and remain in despair, there exists a sense that hopelessness and hunger are imprisoning forces for black Americans. Thus, through his depiction of a black, godlike "Savior," the protagonist reveals how a certain segment of the black population in New York and in Chicago acquired a sense of hope and found the will to survive the oppressive domination experienced from without. For the protagonist, the hypnotic effect of the voice of Marian Anderson and his repetitive encounters with hunger, hopelessness, despair, and racism in the Americas prompt him to act: "Seeing that multitude march past, sharing the concert, privately my mind went back to the initiation of my trip and they began to march by before my soul's eyes, another multitude, this one more gigantic than the one observed. . . ." (Viendo desfilar aquella multitud, privado de compartir el concierto, mi mente se remontó a la iniciación de mi viaje y comenzaron a desfilar ante los ojos del alma otra multitud mucho más gigantesca que la que observaba. . . . *He visto,* 369). His response is to the "American" systemic disenfranchisement and hunger experienced in geographical spaces familiar to him. As the protagonist listens to the swelling crescendos of Marian Anderson while contemplating the multitude, stream-of-conscious thoughts overtake him. In this state, he journeys through South America, Central America, and Mexico; and, with each mental visit, be it to Panama, Guatemala, or Mexico, the number of those admiring the triumphant voice of Marian Anderson grows. For the protagonist, these additions to the multitude assembled represent exploited workers in Panama, poor blacks of the Choco, banana tree plantation workers in Costa Rica. His thoughts become emblematic of a continuum as they link the plight of the oppressed in the Americas. This plight is one filled with despair, death, gloom, exploitation, and hunger, American-style. The protagonist's errant thoughts continue:

> . . . at the end of this caravan of beggars that extended from South America to the U.S.A., the ghosts of the Bowery, sick Harlem and the basements of the Mills Hotel, trembling from the cold, stimulated by the lice. All of them extended their supplicant hands, they looked at me with inexpressive eyes and shouted in my ears: —What does it serve you to travel so much if now you forget us? Why so much dreaming and visiting our huts? Why did you enter the poor cabin asking for shelter if your pen does not curse our pain?

> (... al final de esta caravana de mendigos que se extendía de la América del Sur hasta los EE.UU., los espectros del Bowery, del Harlem enfermo y de los sótanos del Mills's Hotel, temblorosos de frío, acicateados por los

piojos. Todos ellos extendían sus manos suplicantes, me miraban con ojos inexpresivos y me gritaban a los oídos: —¿De qué te sirve tanto viajar si ahora nos olvidas? ¿Para qué tanto soñar y visitar nuestras chozas? ¿Por qué entraste a la cabaña pobre a solicitar abrigo si tu pluma no maldice nuestro dolor?) (*He visto*, 369)

The resolution to the queries of the imagined multitude concludes with the protagonist, as he becomes the elected drum major for the cause of remembrance. He is instructed on his role and unabatedly assumes it as the crescendos continue to stimulate and incite a fire of protest and resistance in his soul:

> You are one of us, remember of your grandmother, a tobacco roller; your aunts living under broken ceilings through which the stars are contemplated; your mother who never has been able to visit a transatlantic one, one of her smallest ambitions of a woman who has seen the sea from childhood. Look well, today you cannot, in spite of your great affliction to listen to the Anderson that is ours, insulted by the same ones that listen to her. Yeah! Go ahead! Swear that from today, wherever you find yourself, under whatever threat you will fight for us. The applause in the interior of the theater erased from my mind that hallucination and already conscious of my acts, I said with all my forces: —Yes, I swear it!

> (Tú eres de nosotros, acuérdate de tu abuela, dobladora de tabaco; de tus tías viviendo bajo techos rotos a través de los cuales se contemplan las estrellas; de tu madre que nunca ha podido visitar un trasatlántico, una de sus poquísimas ambiciones de mujer que ha visto el mar desde la infancia. Fíjate, hoy no puedes, a pesar de tu gran aflicción escuchar a la Anderson que es de los nuestros, insultada por los mismos que la escuchan. Ea! ¡Ándate! Jura que desde hoy, en donde quiera que te encuentres, bajo cualquiera amenaza, lucharás por nosotros. Los aplausos en el interior del teatro borraron de mi mente aquella alucinación y ya consciente de mis actos, dije con todas mis fuerzas: —¡Sí, lo juro!) (*He visto*, 369–70)

From this point onward, the protagonist becomes more propagandistic in his writings, more graphic in unveiling the harsh realities of the poor, especially those mainly of African descent.

He visto is a literary turning point for both author and protagonist. It represents a midcentury exposé of racism in the Americas as well as the presentation of black realities in the United States and in other places of the African diaspora. *He visto* and its companion text, *Pasión*, introduce themes that will be amplified in *Changó*.

Chapter III

La Calle 10, En Chimá, and Chambacú

The "Boom" in Colombian Violence, Hunger, Resistance, and Hope

The decade of the 1960s in Hispanic letters constitutes a transitional period between regionalism and global postmodernism. This theoretical and spatial shift in literature reflects change in thematic concerns that gradually move beyond the boundaries of "home." Commonly referred to as the "Boom," this movement created a wider readership for Latin American works translated into numerous languages. Common to works categorized under the Boom were plots structured around incidents outside the Spanish-speaking world. For many writers like Manuel Zapata Olivella, literary globalization was hardly a novel idea. As seen in *He visto* and *Pasión*, the fictional trajectory of the protagonist crossed *fronteras culturales* as early as the 1950s. In both these texts geographical spaces extend beyond the topographical limitations of his native Colombia. As Zapata Olivella's novelistic boundaries expand, the thematic focus broadens. Thus, it is no surprise that many of his works published during the Boom and even his post-Boom works take on an increasingly international perspective, particularly relative to the African diaspora.

The literary production of Manuel Zapata Olivella from 1960 to 1970 flourished. In this decade alone, he wrote four fictional works: *La Calle 10* (1960), *Detrás el rostro* (1962), *En Chimá* (1963),[1] and *Chambacú* (1967).[2] Zapata Olivella's dramatic works included *Los pasos del indio* (1961), *El cirujano y la selva* (1962), *Tres veces la muerte* (1964), *Caronete liberado* (1964), *Los tres monedas de oro* (1966), and *El retorno a Caín* (1967). His

1. Translated in 1991 by Thomas E. Kooreman as *A Saint Is Born in Chima*.
2. Richard Jackson notes in *Black Writers in Latin America* that this work was first published in Cuba in 1963 as *Corral de negros*. Additionally, it is the first English translation of a work by Manuel Zapata Olivella. Translated in 1989 by Jonathan Tittler as *Chambacu, Black Slum*.

two volumes of short stories, *Cuentos de muerte y libertad* (1961) and *¿Quién dio el fúsil a Oswald?* were critically acclaimed. Zapata Olivella also published three essays, the first of which, "La nueva novela hispanoamericana ante Europa," appeared in *Boletín Cultural Biblioteca Luis A. Arango* in 1962. Next he published "Los milagros de un paralítico: 'Un santo en busca de iglesia,'" an essay about his own fiction, in 1963. The period from 1960 to 1970 represents an "explosion" in the literary production of Manuel Zapata Olivella. It was his most productive decade as a writer, a period that ensures his reputation as a major contributor to Spanish American letters and a seminal figure in the Afro-Hispanic literary canon.

La Calle 10 continues the literary aesthetic of fictionalizing regional history that began with *Tierra*. As Marvin Lewis states, Zapata Olivella's first published work of this decade "is political to the degree that it places fictional characters in a clear historical frame that facilitates our interpretation of reality."[3] It seems safe then, to assume that the fictional characters presented in *La Calle 10* are literary representations of those who experienced the social, political, and historical moments narrated in the text.

LA CALLE 10

Manuel Zapata Olivella's first work of the decade is engulfed in violence, a reflection of the turbulent times. As Raymond Williams notes, violent fiction was a sign of the times:

> During this period the political dialogue was effected predominately in novels of La Violencia, a type of fictionalization so prevalent in the 1950s and 1960s that until the advent of García Márquez's Macundo, the contemporary novel in Colombia was virtually synonymous to "the novela of La Violencia." Over forty such works were published during this period.[4]

Many critics of contemporary Colombian literature cite the preponderance of violence in works such as Zapata Olivella's *La Calle 10* (1960), García Márquez's *La mala hora* (1962), and Mejia Vallejo's *El dia senalado* (1963). Undergirding this focus on aggression in Colombian lit-

---

3. Lewis, *Treading the Ebony Path*, 98.
4. Williams, *Colombian Novel*, 49.

erature is the decadence of the Costa aristocracy, which was accompanied by vicious spasms of national violence. Yvonne Captain-Hidalgo offers an explanation of the violence in *La Calle 10:*

> A partial explanation of this might lie in the specific context of the social concerns of the novel. *Tenth Street* falls clearly in the tradition of the novel of *la violencia* in Colombia because it speaks to a period of violent struggle in Colombia history in which the assassination of the political leader Jorge Eliecar Gaitan played an important part. Much of the literature stemming from this moment in the country's history would place emphasis on Bogotá or at least major cities where the immediate impact of the violence was most evident, which explains the shift from a rural setting to an urban one in the novel. As a direct consequence, the question of leadership undergoes revision.[5]

As Captain-Hidalgo explains, the violence that saturates the narrative framework of *La Calle 10* reflects the political unrest experienced in Bogotá and other Colombian locales prior to and during the decade of the 1960s. Thus, as a literary transition from historical reality to fictional representation, *La Calle 10* violently opens with the first section of this bifurcated text: "La semilla," or "The Seed," which functions symbolically. What is "sown" sets the foundation for what will be "reaped" in the second half of the novel, "La cosecha," or "The Harvest."

"La semilla" begins with the violent screams of a man who finds the corpse of a woman who has been "assassinated," gunned down on Tenth Street. She is identified as Saturnina, the wife of the distraught Pelúo. Consistent with Zapata Olivella's prior works, this text focuses on a nuclear family. Poverty, hunger, and violence emerge as themes. The reader learns that Saturnina's death is a result of robbery. The resolute act of robbery, then, becomes the means by which these residents attempt to improve their lives. Those who suffer from poverty are obliged to commit illicit acts in order to ameliorate their social position and feed their hunger. Poverty surfaces early in the novel as Pelúo bemoans his inability to offer his wife a "proper" burial. He is forced to venture into the heart of Tenth Street in search of an adequate container in which to commit the remains of his beloved wife. So poor is Pelúo that he has lost the habit of using money (. . . había perdido el hábito de usar dinero, *La Calle 10,* 14). The melancholy fog that veils Tenth Street is

---

5. Captain-Hidalgo, *Culture of Fiction,* 64.

evidenced by the horror and sadness of Pelúo's son as he embraces his dead mother while Pelúo begins the search for a burial box.

Hunger is an obsessive leitmotif that unifies the work. Vivid depictions of men, women, children, and dogs who scavenge for food are encountered from the initial pages of the novel. Epaminondas, the celibate wanderer, is first introduced to the reader in connection with his mule "Desprecio" (Scorn, Disdain). Epaminondas found the mule starved and wounded by beatings from his "primitive" owners, who allowed him to escape. The affinity between man and mule creates a familiar bond, and he and Desprecio act as a kind of couple as they roam the marketplace that dissects Tenth Street. But, it is Parmenio's family that constitutes the central focus of the narrative plot. Through the introduction of the members of his family, the reader discovers the depths to which one will descend in order to survive. The family consists of Parmenio's wife, Teolinda, his daughter, Ruperta, his son, Gabriel, and a host of other children collectively referred to as "los Pulgas" or "fleas." The interconnection between man and his environment is intimate and disgusting. Readers feel the filth and decay of Tenth Street as it is revealed through the characters. The reference to the children of Parmenio as "fleas," introduces an esperpentic element of the carnivalesque and the grotesque. Children are presented as scavengers, wandering errantly with stray dogs and other helpless animals in search of money and food. Their Sunday morning ritual consists of getting to the church doors early enough to beg from worshippers and return home with money to help sustain the family. Hyperbolic hunger is ever-present and ever-worsening. Parmenio is forced to admit there exists today more hunger than yesterday (hay más hambre que ayer. *La Calle 10*, 12). The household of Parmenio is an emblematic manifestation of the hunger, violence, malfeasance, and filth of *La Calle 10*.

Race and ethnic mixing are also explored through the characterization of Parmenio's family. His wife, Teolinda, is a member of an indigenous tribe and is commonly referred to as *india*, or Indian woman. She is described as having long black hair and a brown complexion. Parmenio views his whiteness as a liability. He wishes that he and his children were phenotypically more like their mother: "It bothered him that he was white. He would have preferred to be like Teolinda. His children would not have gotten that white color and reddish hair, which prevents them from blending into the crowd." (Se incomodó de que él fuera blanco. Hubiera querido ser como Teolinda. Sus hijos no habrían sacado ese color blancuzco y los pelos rojos que les impedían confundirse entre la muchedumbre. *La Calle 10*, 14) Parmenio's frustration, his desire to blend in with his downtrodden neighbors could be a result of the acceptance of his marginalized social status. He sees that his whiteness is negated by his marriage to Teolinda. His union to an Indian limits not only his social mobility, but also that of his children. His marriage to Teolinda ensures his degradation, symbolized by their sharing a rotten orange extracted from dirty water. Because of her pregnancy, she can no longer earn money for the family, and Parmenio describes her as a loafer. Teolinda spends most nights begging from drunken men in the local watering hole.

Women are portrayed as negatively as natives. Like her mother, Teolinda, Ruperta is presented against a backdrop of incest, sexual pillage, and prostitution. Her entrance into womanhood pleases Parmenio ("finally they will be able to"), who takes encouragement from the fact that his daughter is developing physically. Her maturing breasts indicate to Parmenio her readiness to join her mother in the effort to relieve the family's hunger (Ya es una mujercita! *La Calle 10*, 13) Ruperta's first sexual encounter is depicted more as rape than prostitution. She appears helpless, confused, and unable to interject her will. Her assailant, Sátiro, who is described as an old man, "el viejo," lures her with a piece of cheese, which reminds her of her younger brother's hunger: "From the bar a hand appeared offering her a piece of cheese. Ruperta did not know what to do, she would have liked to flee, disappear from his sight. The cheese reminded her of her brother's hunger. She smiled." (Por el mostrador se asomó una mano ofreciéndole un pedazo de queso. Ruperta no supo qué hacer, le habría gustado huir, perderse de su vista. El queso le recordó que su hermanito tenía hambre. Sonrió. *La Calle 10*, 74) Clearly, it is Ruperta's desire to eradicate the hunger of her family that motivates her surrender:

> Ruperta, hardly thirteen years old, had had to personally confront the family's tragedy. Her little twin brothers were crying begging for food; her mother was feeling strong labor pains indicating the imminence of birth, and her father, bedridden from despair, was slipping away from reality, more aggressively than ever.

> (Ruperta, sin haber cumplido todavía los trece años, había tenido que apersonarse de la tragedia de la familia. Sus hermanitos gemelos lloraban solicitando alimento; su madre sentía fuertes dolores en el vientre

que anunciaban la inminencia del parto, y su padre, acostado por la des-
peración, se abstraía de la realidad, más agresiva que nunca.) (*La Calle
10*, 55)

The use of cheese as bait recalls an earlier incident involving Ruperta
and a rat. While seated, she sees a rat run across the floor. Reacting out
of fear, she seeks Sátiro for protection and refuge. Sátiro will later use
rat food, cheese, to bait and entrap Ruperta, as if she were a rodent.
The inference here is that women are nonhuman and valueless. This
perspective engenders the gross abuse suffered by women in the novel.
As the episode with Ruperta and Sátiro reveals, Ruperta is simply too
hungry to resist Sátiro's gropes: "Suppressing her, the old man's hot
arm roamed over her body; her hands were held down. . . . She did not
have the breath to resist." (Sofocándola, el brazo caliente del viejo
recorría su cuerpo; sus manos apretaban. . . . No tenía aliento para re-
sistir. *La Calle 10*, 74). The narrator indicates that Ruperta desired to
scream, close her legs and flee, but she lacked the will power to do so
(Quiso gritar, cerrar sus piernas, herir aquella boca que la lamía, pero
no tuvo voluntad. *La Calle 10*, 74–75) This encounter with Sátiro marks
Ruperta's initiation into the world of prostitution as a means of survival. For the majority of the women that inhabit the confines of Tenth
Street, prostitution is a necessary evil.

As the novel progresses, the themes of protest and social revolution
that are common to Olivella's work come to the forefront. Tamayo, the
Artist, and the black ex-boxer Mamatoco advocate change and social
protest. As editors of a local newspaper, "Voz del Pueblo" (The voice of
the people), Tamayo and Mamatoco voice their criticism of the government and engender social unrest when their fellow citizens begin to
react to their oppression, hunger, and neglect. The newspaper becomes
the vehicle by which the propaganda of the revolution is disseminated
to the people. As the first section of the novel ends and hunger intensifies, the articles published in "Voz del Pueblo" implicate the government for the squalor of Tenth Street and set the stage for the people's
protest: "The people will not only accuse the guilty ones, but will take
justice in their own hands. Bastards, you don't know the vindictive rage
of the common masses." (El pueblo no sólo acusará a los cupables, sino
que tomará justicia por sus propios manos. ¡Miserables, ustedes no
conocen la ira vindicatoria de las masas populares! *La Calle 10*, 63) This
revolt is motivated by policemen who, in an effort to subdue a growing

mob, engage in a shooting spree that kills Mamatoco and critically wounds Tamayo, the voices of the revolt. As all hell breaks loose on Tenth Street, ambulance sirens drown out the bullets of the police, the wails of the injured and the agitation of the mob. Tamayo promises revenge to the very end, even to death:

> The assassins try to hide their crime with new victims! . . . The plan of the Government is to drown hunger with bullets, but the people will know how to drown the Government with the blood from its own crimes! . . . Organize the defense! . . . Down with the assassins! . . . Long live the "Voice of the People"! I solemnly swear before our rage that the newspaper will continue denouncing the crimes of the Government, even when it costs me my life. . . .
>
> (¡Los asesinos tratan de ocultar su crimen con nuevas víctimas! ... El plan del Gobierno es ahogar el hambre con balas, pero el pueblo sabrá ahogar al Gobierno con la sangre de sus propios crímenes! ... ¡Organicemos la defensa! ... ¡Abajo los asesinos! ¡Viva "La Voz del Pueblo"! ¡Yo juro solemnemente, ante vuestra ira, que el periódico continuará denunciando los crímenes del Gobierno, aun cuando me cueste la vida....) (*La Calle 10*, 79)

Tamayo incites an insurrection with these words. It is at this moment that the concluding section of the novel, "La cosecha" (The Harvest), begins.

The second section of the novel depicts the harvest of the seeds of protest planted in the first. The first words of the chapter call for the death and destruction of the corrupt government and its minion assassins (¡Abajo el mal gobierno! . . . Muera el mal gobierno! *La Calle 10*, 83). This outcry is a reaction to the brutal deaths of Mamatoco and others. As in the opening chapter of the work, violence on Tenth Street is pointedly in evidence. With rifles and provincial weapons in hand, the people take to the streets in order to assert power. In a kind of civil war, the oppressed meet their oppressors with one goal in mind: liberation. A major contributor to the people's effort is Rengifo, a rebellious police officer whose participation in the liberation underscores the corruption in the state he betrays.

A consistent reminder of the ills of the establishment is *la Facultad de la Medicina,* or the medical school. From the beginning, the reader is aware of the enmity between the community of slum dwellers and this icon of their oppression and destruction. References to this social institution are interwoven throughout the text as the unwilling and unknowing wounded are rounded up and hauled off to the facility, where they will be slaughtered for the advancement of medicine. In the first chapter, we find Pelúo desperately trying to reclaim the body of his wife before she is taken to the medical school. So intense is the fear of the school that Parmenio would prefer that his pregnant wife deliver on the streets, which she ultimately does. Both man and beast become subjects for in vivo experiments for training medical students. As the revolt escalates, so does the number of casualties, and the hospital of the medical school becomes as chaotic and brutal as Tenth Street.

As the novel concludes, the emphasis is placed on the consequences of the revolt. Graphic narrative descriptions depict the manner in which the dead blanket the terrain of Tenth Street. Looters and revolutionaries pass over these bodies as if they were a natural part of the pavement, demonstrating the lack of value and regard for human life that permeates this street lined with desolation, despair, and insatiable "hunger." Yet, consistent with the narrative aesthetic in many of the works of Zapata Olivella, there is hope in the end. The children that survive the revolt and those that are born on the new Tenth Street will benefit from the upheaval:

> Parmenio breathed strength and optimism that he never knew. The fortitude demonstrated by the people contaminated him with a limitless confidence in their own strength. He knew he was able to destroy the bars of any warehouse, to handle with ability a gun and even to commanding the crowds. His son also would be a warrior and for that reason instead of being called Gabriel as his wife wished, he would be called "Mamatoco."

> (Parmenio respiraba fuerzas y optimismo que jamás conoció. El poderío demonstrado por el pueblo, lo contagió de una confianza ilímite en sus propias fuerzas. Se sabía capaz de destrozar los barrotes de cualquier bodega, de manejar con habilidad un fusil y hasta de comandar las turbas. Su hijo también sería aguerrido y por eso en vez de llamarse Gabriel como deseaba su mujer, le daría el nombre de "Mamatoco.") (*La Calle 10*, 120)

The symbolic naming of the child in honor of one of the slain revolutionaries assures the continuity of the people's struggle; the spirit of the revolution is passed on through the process of naming. Parmenio gains strength in the thought that his child represents the gratitude and vigilance of many generations of the poor and oppressed. The narrative voice indicates that Parmenio is well aware of the fact that the fight for civil justice and the eradication of hunger is a continual one. But, largely due to the will exhibited by the people, Parmenio is hopeful that the struggle will continue until the manifestations of societal hunger are ended. The poet Tamayo who urges Rengifo, the renegade policeman, to keep his weapon, echoes these sentiments. Distraught by his unsuccessful search for his love Chava, Rengifo laments the possibility that she is among the dead. The poet informs him that government forces have overtaken the city and are shooting at all armed persons. Rengifo removes his rifle from his shoulder and attempts to destroy it against the street, but the poet stops him, signifying that the fight for liberation continues: "Keep it, my brother, for tomorrow, very soon, we will need it!" (¡Guárdalo, hermano, mañana, muy pronto, lo necesitaremos! *La Calle 10*, 124)

La Calle 10 is a clear novelistic representation of the social and political situation of Zapata Olivella's native Colombia during the 1960s, when violence overtook the streets of many Colombian cities. *La Calle 10* then, reflects the plight of poor, dispossessed Colombians and their effort to alter their mode of existence. Like the works of fiction that precede it, the major themes of *La Calle 10* include poverty, oppression, hunger, isolation, marginalization, revolution, race/ethnicity, and the eternal hope that conditions will improve.

En Chimá, nace un santo

En Chimá is the work of the 1960s to receive the most attention by literary critics. Even so, there is not much scholarship on the text. Although its "place" in contemporary Latin American literature is beginning to be defined, critics have yet to devote much-needed analytical attention to this work. In one of the few articles published on *En Chimá*, Marvin Lewis notes that, despite the fact that Zapata Olivella had already written six novels, "one is hard pressed to find half a dozen articles on the author's works."[6]

En Chimá is geographically located in a marginalized Colombian town located in the Sinú region near the city of Lorica. As in other works, the protagonists are poor, a fact underscored by Marvin Lewis:

---

6. Lewis, *Treading the Ebony Path*, 145.

"Zapata Olivella's most successful novels describe isolated villages and communities where people are victims of poverty, fanaticism and violence."[7]

Zapata Olivella was born in Lorica in 1920, creating an intimate bond between the author and the text. This emphasis on poverty surfaces in *En Chimá* when the narrative focus is placed on the community's lack of material necessities, hope, and freedom. The citizens of Chimá are poor and oppressed, and it appears that the only possibility for change lies in their belief in the "miracles" of an invalid whom they want to sanctify. For this destitute and fanatical population, the invalid becomes a symbol of hope.

As exemplified in many of the Boom novels, magical realism and temporal fragmentation are central to the narrative development. *En Chimá* is structured around the Vidal family, the paralytic Domingo Vidal in particular. The characters constitute oppressed, poor, and marginalized people whose oppressed social condition forces them to place their hope in Domingo Vidal. The protagonist's name, "Sunday," evokes a sense of religious symbolism that contributes to his divinely acquired status. Thomas Kooreman suggests that the socioeconomic conditions of the citizens of Chimá make them vulnerable: "Poverty and hunger drove the people of Chimá to seek refuge in the supposed miracles of a paralytic boy, Domingo Vidal."[8] In their quest for material relief, the people place their faith in Domingo and his presumed miracles. This optimism is manifested in the lives of four central characters: Andrea, Eduviges, las gemelas (twins) de Anachárico, and Camilo. These characters also serve to develop one of Olivella's major themes: the triumph of popular cultural beliefs and practices over those deemed mainstream or "official."

The first "miracle" involves the rescue of Domingo, the invalid son of the widow Rafaela, by Father Berrocal, the parish priest. This rescue from a burning hut is viewed as miraculous by the people because neither Father Berrocal nor Domingo are burned upon emerging from the flames. Thus, the people deem this the first miracle performed by their self-appointed parochial saint: "To their general surprise, neither Domingo nor his clothing was burned. Miracle! Miracle!" (Para sorpresa

---

7. Ibid.
8. Thomas Kooreman, "*Pasión vagabunda,* comienzo de una creación ficcionesca," 6.

general, a Domingo ni siquiera se le ha quemado la ropa. —¡Milagro! ¡Milagro! *En Chima*, 12) This initial miracle causes many villagers to evoke the assistance of Domingo and his unexplainable powers in alleviating the pain in their wretched lives. Hence, Domingo Vidal surfaces as the central character, one who embodies the "magical" in an otherwise abject reality. The question then becomes, who is actually responsible for these miraculous outcomes? Is it the Invalid or the protection provided through the "collar" of the parish priest? Domingo Vidal and Father Berrocal thus reflect binary conflict between popular and official allegiances weighing on the dwellers of Chimá.

The second miracle involves Vidal's sisters, Andrea and Balaude. Andrea, the elder of the two, is positioned as the maternal, spinster archetype whose major concern is her family. She is unable to conceive; thus, she devotes all of her energy to caring for her brother, Domingo. He becomes her surrogate child, whom she regards as her own son: "she covers Domingo and grooms him as if he were a rag doll. She hugs him and dreams about having him nurse from her own breast. A child, born obsessively from her womb." (empolva a Domingo y le acicala como si fuera una muñeca de trapo. La abraza y cree tenerle en su propio seno. Un hijo que le nace obsesivamente en su útero. *En Chimá*, 13) Through caring for her brother, Andrea finds purpose and hope in life. However, they are warped manifestations of purpose and hope in light of that fact that they constitute fanatical responses of desperate characters toward a pathetic and paralyzed invalid who is incapable of tending to his own needs. The irony is that Domingo, who inspires a sense of fulfillment and hope in others, is given an independent role in the narrative. The reader is only presented with a peripheral view of this invalid whose voice is never privileged in the novel.

Balaude, the antithesis of her sister, Andrea, is outraged by the physical incapacitation of her younger brother. She refuses to accept the fact that he is physically challenged. She forces him to try and walk and to be a "man": "I wish that above all you were a man who had lots of children and fight with a machete against the toughest men of the village." (Quisiera que fuera todo un hombre: que tuviera muchos hijos y peleara a machete con los más forzudos del pueblo. *En Chimá*, 14) Balaude views her brother as less than human and searches for a mechanism by which he can overcome his limitations. Seeing that he is unable to comply with her desires, she insists he draw a picture of the Virgin Mary. He sketches an indiscernible object, but Balaude becomes convinced that it is the Holy Virgin. The villagers all hurry to behold this new miracle and are amazed at the work of this thirty-year-old, immobile paralytic. The village sacristan, Jeremías, races to the scene in order to give sacred testament to the drawing. It is significant that Jeremías rather than Father Berrocal is cast as the guarantor in order to develop the conflict between that which is "official" and that which is "popular" for the people of Chimá. Upon seeing the etching, Jeremías declares that it indeed is the Virgin Mary, fueling thusly the fanaticism of villagers who proclaim the drawing a miracle and Domingo a saint.

The miraculous sketch of the invalid engenders more than hope. Anselmo and Eduviges have been unable to conceive and are desperate for a child. Domingo Vidal becomes their last resort. Taking the relic of the invalid, Eduviges places it on her stomach, and within a few days she conceives. Upon hearing that Eduviges is with child, the Chimaleros hail the event as yet another miracle. Miracle and magical realism again converge as Domingo is called to rid the daughters of the unfortunate Anichárico of their sexual encounters with the folkloric goblin Juan Lara. Anichárico, in an act of hopelessness and desperation, takes the girls to Domingo in order to exorcise their demons. In a ritualistic manner similar to the biblical depiction of Mary and Martha, the girls gather around the Invalid's feet, kiss his hands three times, and recite seven Hail Mary's. The number three recalls the trinity; the number seven represents perfection and completion. After performing the ritual, the possessed girls' spirits are purified, and the night visits of Juan Lara cease. For the villagers of Chimá, Domingo is elevated to a Christlike figure who cures the sick, impregnates the barren, and casts out demons. As Marvin Lewis suggests:

> The Chimaleros' creation and construction of the myth of Domingo Vidal is based on the archetype of Christ and on biblical mythology. He is a symbolic projection of their hopes and values, and he binds the community together in its many moments of crisis. They do need an immediate source of strength for the daily hardships that they must face and also provides them the impetus for rebellion. Domingo temporarily fills this need.[9]

Domingo indeed surfaces as the "savior" of the Chimaleros. Like Jesus Christ, he brings peace and hope to the desolate world of Chimá. In

9. Lewis, *Treading the Ebony Path*, 96.

line with biblical imagery, Domingo, like Jesus, dies at the age of thirty-three. As a final tribute to the life of their "savior," the villagers wish to name him the patron saint of Chimá.

En Chimá plunges the reader into the depths of magical realism not only through the miraculous deeds of the invalid of Chimá, but also through the oral tradition that prescribes the region's folklore. The opening scene depicts Latin American "magic realism" at its best through the literary depiction of the celebrated Day of the Dead. This entire scene captures the essence of the people's faith in these popular, "supernatural" happenings. Raymond Williams states:

> *En Chimá nace un santo* (1964), set in the region of the Sinú and the towns of Chimá and Lorica, relates stories of the Costa's prodigious happenings and captures some of the magic of this oral culture before it was popularized internationally by García Márquez. Zapata Olivella is aware of the specialness of the culture he is fictionalizing, beginning with an epigraph on myths in primitive cultures. The story concerns religious fanaticism, but to depict the cultural milieu the author juxtaposes the superstitious and magical religion of an oral culture with the official tradition of writing culture.[10]

The "prodigious happenings" alluded to by Williams are the "miracles" performed by the invalid, Domingo Vidal. His ability to heal and to cast out demons became indisputable feats for the dwellers of Chimá. Clearly, Manuel Zapata Olivella's folklorist attachment resonates throughout this work. As William states, Zapata Olivella portrays the cultural milieu of this small town through an oral narration that fuels and sustains the superstitious and magical beliefs of the parishioners. Magic realism relies on the wind-carried echoes of verbal murmurings to inspire belief.

Manuel Zapata Olivella's fiction establishes an antithetical paradigm whereby official and popular religious practices coexist. This syncretic combination of Roman Catholicism and local superstition creates conflict for official religious representatives. However, the narrative voice concludes that the current amalgam of religious rites is best for the people: "Superstition and religiosity are two contradictory concepts that complement each other." (La superstición y la religiosidad son dos contradictorios que se complementan. *En Chimá*, 53) Within the text, religious superstition is linked to the concept of magical realism. Nontraditional

10. Williams, *Colombian Novel*, 115.

practices are perceived as surreal customary habits deeply entrenched within the cultural beliefs of the people. This complementary relationship between religion and magic realism in the lives of the Chimaleros creates conflict when superstition and religion collide.

On the Day of the Dead, villagers arrive at the cemetery to commune with their deceased relatives. During this religious observation, the congenial joining of religion and superstition is everywhere in evidence:

> Those who have come walking for many nights through mire and mountains join their relatives of the village. Religiously, they make their annual visit to the dead. Drilling their knees in the mud, they bless themselves and begin to relate to their dead the happenings that took place during the year as if the dead were listening to them. . . . Today is the day of the Dead. The deceased clean their remains, decorate themselves with their shrouds and with the same vanity of country girls, they adorn their scalped heads with heliotropic flowers picked in the fields at midnight. Squatting, with the joints of their tibias crossed and with their insides empty, the deceased receive their bereaved with a big smile.

> (A los deudos del pueblo se suman quienes han venido andando desde noches atrás por entre cenagales y montañas. Cumplen religiosamente la vista anual a sus muertos. Clavando sus rodillos en el barro, se santiguan y les cuentan lo acaecido durante el año como si les escucharan.... Hoy, día de difundos, los muertos limpian sus propias osamentos, se engalanan con los sudarios y, con la misma coquetería de las muchachas campesinas, se adoran la rapada cabeza con flores de cabalonga y heliotropos, recogidas en los campos a medianoche. En cuclillas, cruzados los canutos de sus tibias y con las cuencas vacías, los finados reciben a sus dolientes con una sonrisa desjarretada.) (*En Chimá*, 7–8)

The point of cultural contestation arises when this conversation with the dead suggests an impaired state of reality. The Chimaleros actually believe that their dead have been resurrected in order to speak with them, as if they were visiting incarcerated family members. Equally hallucinatory is the manner in which the deceased are described during their own preparation to visit with family members. The dead walk, talk, clean and dress themselves, pick flowers, and reincarnate for the visit with their loved ones. These "supernatural" occurrences are directly linked to magical realism in that they are viewed by outside observers as magical, surrealistic, and marvelously beyond the natural. However, for those within, these "happenings" are perceived as a normal and natural part of their reality. There is no manipulation of physical "place" in that the cemetery does not take on fantastic symbolic value for the Chimaleros. However, the occurrences that take place, like Domingo's miracles, are fantastic for the reader. As the novel progresses, this dichotomy between the real and the fantastic becomes the ultimate cause of religious conflict when the practices of the people confront the dominant construct of organized religion.

An early conflict occurs when Father Berrocal, the official parish priest, comes to Chimá after having received notice of the religious fanaticism of the people regarding the miracles of Dominguito. Father Berrocal is taken aback as he witnesses the villagers praising Domingo and referring to him as Santo Domingo. The followers of Domingo inform the father of the many miracles performed by their patron saint. Berrocal becomes outraged and deems their behavior blasphemous and pagan. The father then denounces the sainthood of the invalid and destroys the sketch of the Holy Virgin. The Chimaleros believe that it is the priest who has blasphemed and committed a heretic act against their "saint": "The parish priest observes the drawing and holds it against the light. Finally he rips it to shreds and throws away the pieces. . . . The villagers cross each other in a frenzy and fall to their knees overcome with terror. The priest commits apostasy." (El párroco observa el dibujo, lo vuelve contra la luz. Finalmente lo desgarra contrariado y arroja los pedazos. . . . Se persignan y arrodillan sobrecogidos depavor. El sacerdote incurre en apostasía. *En Chimá*, 41) In the view of Domingo's followers, Father Berrocal has renounced their religious belief. The priest, on the other hand, does not doubt that the people have reverted to paganism. Thus, the harmonious coexistence of popular and official religious practices comes to an end when Father Berrocal insists that the people petition Saint Emidgio, the officially ordained patron saint of Chimá, for forgiveness. As the people surrender and temporarily abandon popular practices, collective hope is diminished. In the interim, the sacristan Jeremías converts to the cult of Domingo, begins a crusade to honor the miraculous actions of Domingo, and sells prayers as if he were a missionary. For Jeremías and the other citizens of Chimá and surrounding towns, their worship of Domingo is not intended as a total rejection of Catholicism. They have merely altered traditional Catholicism to make it more culturally relevant to their situation. To them, Saint Domingo provides the tangible hope that Saint Emidgio never could. Unlike their "officially" appointed saint, Domingo can be physically seen and touched. His miracles are also tangibly experienced.

After Domingo's death, conflict between popular and official religion intensifies. The Chimaleros are confident that their proclaimed saint has departed to sit at the side of God. But, because of the pagan beliefs exhibited by his followers, the Church denies Domingo a religious burial. Consequently, Jeremías and the other followers of Domingo take the cadaver to the cemetery for burial. Symbolically, the refusal to allow the remains of Domingo into the church represents an act of hegemonic suppression of the beliefs of the people. Thus, two years later, the villagers, again under the direction of Jeremías, return to the cemetery on Easter to finally give him a burial more befitting a saint. Upon exhuming the body, they discover water in the tomb and are convinced that it is holy water. Additionally, they note that Domingo's body has not decomposed. It is as lifelike as if he were still alive and in a deep, peaceful sleep. In the minds of those assembled, these facts bear witness to his sainthood. As a result, their desire to sanctify him is renewed.

The biblical parallels and symbolism are quite evident. Like Mary the mother of Jesus and Mary Magdalene, the people go to the tomb in search of the body of their "savior." The miracle of the Resurrection is paralleled by the discovery of holy water and an unblemished cadaver. For the people, however, popular religion will triumph over Christianity. In a rejection of hegemonic religious practices, the villagers remove the statue of the official saint from the altar and replace it with the body of Domingo. Popular religion is victorious in Chimá. As the novel ends, Father Berrocal returns to Chimá in a final attempt to redeem the villagers and restore "official" religious order. He and other officials from Lorica remove Domingo's body from the church, return it to the cemetery, and quarter it. The father delivers a fire-and-brimstone sermon guaranteeing damnation to those who forsake the teachings of Christianity, and he forces many villagers to repent. He is on the verge of reestablishing Christianity when he dies, and the people see his death as the revenge of Saint Domingo. Religious officials from Lorica come to Chimá to restore order. In the violence that ensues, Jeremías is killed. The people declare him a prophet of Saint Domingo, and they continue to practice their popular brand of religion. The hope of the Chimaleros is restored as they proclaim the birth of a saint in Chimá.

En Chimá is a text about religion, but it is a religion that is manipulated and subverted by the virus of neocolonialism. Neocolonialism, masked in religious hegemony, is an integral component of this novel. The subjugated dwellers of Chimá are denied religious expression as they try to sanctify one of their own. Power, authority, and social order are relegated from without, in the figure of Father Berrocal, the symbolic representation of the "neocolonial" force that dictates social structure and religious order. Through his sanctioning of official Catholicism, Father Berrocal prevents the people of Chimá from exercising collective, communal power and denies them the authority to govern their own spirituality. Thus, they attempt to liberate themselves by rejecting conventional official practices and revolting violently in order to maintain agency. Of interest is the fact that the primary instigators of the vicious attack on the people of Chimá are Father Berrocal and other officials of the Church. They invade the town and savagely dismember the body of Domingo in an effort to subjugate the people. The result of these encounters reveals the sociopolitical message imbedded in the text. Father Berrocal dies as a result of the violence, and the people attribute his death to the power of Domingo. The people have successfully thwarted colonial power. Such an ending expresses Zapata Olivella's faith in the ability of the oppressed and downtrodden to mount protest and survive.

CHAMBACÚ, CORRAL DE NEGROS

Manuel Zapata Olivella's *Chambacú* is approaching canonical status and is, without doubt, one of Zapata Olivella's best works of fiction. Like *En Chimá*, *Chambacú* is in the tradition of the new novel and the Boom. Many of the narrative strategies of both are contained in this fictional work. In *Chambacú*, the reader witnesses the expansion of the writer's ideology. His focus here is the representation of black Colombians. What sets this work apart and charts a new direction in the literary trajectory of Zapata Olivella is the work's unapologetic emphasis on the social, political, and economic realties of the disenfranchised and poor Afro-Colombians. The novel concerns itself with the "darker" side of the struggle for social equality in Colombia and illustrates the author's progression toward an Afro-Colombian thematic in his work.

Prior to this work, black representation in the South American experience was eclipsed by the emphasis on the poor, indigenous South American. Thus, with the publication of *Chambacú*, Zapata Olivella's narrative focus progresses from the generic to the specific. By this, I mean that his emphasis shifts from a subtle focus on race and ethnicity (*Tierra, La Calle 10,* and *En Chimá*) to a more specific emphasis (*He visto* and *Pasión*). However, in those earlier works, the racial composition of the characters is not fully developed, and it is not linked to the social context of the work.

In earlier works, racism is not intimately linked to their social position. Rather, blacks, poor white Hispanics, and Indians are all presented as equally victimized. The opposite is true with *Chambacú*. From the first lines of the work, the reader confronts a black populace.

As in previous novels, Colombia is the setting of the text. The tiny island of Chambacú is situated off the Caribbean Atlantic coast of Cartegena in the Colombian region of the Chocó. This locale is important because it is the furthermost point off the mainland extending into the ocean. It is connected to the mainland by a bridge that facilitates travel to Cartegena and back. It is also where many Colombians of African ancestry and the region's poorest people reside. Thus, in terms of its geographical space, this community of largely poor black Colombians exists as an isolated island that is literally cut off from the sociopolitical structure that governs it. From this vantage point, *Chambacú* is a neocolonialist work. The novel opens with social and political protest over the lack of basic public services such as sewer, water, and sanitation. As the novel advances, national and international exploitation of the situation further complicates the lives of this regionally identified black population. Their fight for survival reaches a global audience with the decimation and the emasculation of the male population, due to the belligerent efforts of the United States.

In *Chambacú*, Zapata Olivella exposes his readers to a three-tiered spectrum of oppression, exploitation, and subjugation. The first level presents the plight of blacks forced to survive within the confines of their displaced locality. The second level centers on the political fight for equitable treatment and due process supposedly afforded to every citizen of Colombia regardless of racial/ethnic classification or socioeconomic status. However, the reader witnesses the fictional oppression of the majority black population through their fight for equality and their social protest. The final focus of the novel is its international appeal. The government is rounding up the men of the area for the figurative slaughter: the Korean War. The war is presented as a major component of the North American political agenda, one designed to exploit the disenfranchised citizens of developing nations. The exploitation of poor blacks for the benefit of "First World" political powers is a central theme of the work. Thus, the social issues of oppression, subjugation, and exploitation are explored locally, nationally, and internationally. The exploitation within Chambacú, perpetrated by local and U.S. authorities is at center stage in the novel's opening chapter, "Los reclutos" (The recruits), and continues throughout to the concluding chapter, "La batalla" (The battle).

As in the preceding novels, the narrative development surrounds the family unit. *Chambacú* focuses on the plight of the family of La Cotena, the principal matriarch. This unit consists of the mother, her five children, and one grandson: Máximo, the activist; Medialuna, the boxer; Críspulo, the fighting-cock breeder; José Raquel, the assimilationist; and, Clotilde, the domestic worker for rich whites in Manga and the mother of a mestizo son. Through these characters, the reader discovers the social and political dynamic that surrounds Chambacú. The lives and social circumstances of family members reflect the actual struggle of Afro-Colombians from the 1950s to the present day. Interestingly, no surnames are used in this work, providing a more universal appeal to the work while situating it within the novels of the new narrative and the Boom.

La Cotena and her family are emblematic of the larger population of poor and dispossessed blacks scattered throughout the African diaspora. She emerges as a dominant matriarch who worries about the future of her family in Chambacú. She is also politically outspoken. Her views regarding Colombia's involvement in the Korean War are exposed in the first part of the novel. She would rather see her sons dead than have them become assassins in a war, killing people who had done no wrong to them. La Cotena is definitely not a static, monolithic character. Her eldest son, Máximo, shares her ideals. He is a revolutionary and the instigator of social and political change. The reader learns that he had been incarcerated for his political demonstrations and defiant protests. His arrest is central to making him a hero, as Richard Jackson points out:

> Máximo, the activist protagonist in *Chambacú* is perhaps the best known of all of Zapata Olivella's creations. More than any other Afro-Hispanic novel, *Chambacú* is a novel of a place, a ghetto in Colombia to which poor Black people were restricted. Zapata Olivella brings this ghetto to life through Máximo, whose heroic example of civic leadership inspires the slum dwellers to revolt against their sorry conditions.[11]

Jackson's account of Máximo is on the mark. However, his suggestion that *Chambacú* is more a novel of regional locale than other Afro-Hispanic

---

11. Jackson, *Black Writers and the Hispanic Canon*, 52.

novels is worth challenging in light of the emphasis placed on the Sinú River valley basin in *Tierra mojada* and on the fictional village of Chimá in *En Chimá*. The theme of place is always important in the fiction of Zapata Olivella. The author takes a geographical construct, either real or fictitious, and exploits it in order to reveal the story of a people who are intimately tied to it for the purpose of exposing the realities of that people's existence through fiction. Máximo, in addition to his role as a political and social activist, is the bearer and preserver of African history and culture. Ancestral references penetrate the discourse of *Chambacú*, and the essence of their memory is demonstrated through Máximo, who is the studious member of the clan of La Cotena. Máximo's role is critical. He bridges the gap between the exiled Africans at Chambacú and their ancestry. It is also he who keeps alive the history of having been, as Homi Bhabha would refer to it, "gathered" or exiled on the voiceless island of Chambacú:

> It is not by chance that Chambacú, pen of blacks, was born at the foot of the walls. Our ancestors were brought here to build them. The slave ships packed slaves from all parts of Africa. Mandingo, Wolof, Minas, Carablíes, Biáfaras, Yoruba, more than forty tribes.

> (No es ocasional que Chambacú, corral de negros, haya nacido al pie de las murallas. Nuestro antepasados fueron traídos aquí para construirlas. Los barcos negreros llagados atestados de esclavos provenientes de toda Africa. Mandingas, yolofos, minas,carabalíes, biáfaras, yoruba, más que cuarenta tribus.) (*Chambacú*, 189)

Like a great African folklorist, Máximo historically recounts the arrival of Africans to Chambacú. Relying on the inherited oral tradition of the Old World, he reminds others that their ancestors were Africans, brought to the New World and to the island of Chambacú for the purpose of slavery, and that their existence then, as now, is one of exile, exploitation, and abject neglect.

The antithesis of Máximo is his brother José Raquel, the ever-present "black-sheep" of the clan. A member of the Chambacú underground, he smuggles in and sells contraband as a means of escaping the daily gloom and despair. He is, as Richard Jackson reiterates, the counterpart to Máximo: "In a clear case of contrast with the novel's hero, José Raquel is devoid of principle, a slave to pretension, and an example of bad judgment, which he exhibits by turning to the illegal activities he

had perfected during wartime."[12] José Raquel is emblematic of the
male members of society who totally lose faith in the majority community and attempt to secure a future by manipulating and exploiting the
legitimate system. Unlike Máximo, José Raquel has no desire to fight
for the rights of the people. His main concern is himself, as his decisions
bear out. In "Los reclutos," while the majority of the black males of
Chambacú are trying to escape being rounded up for the Colombian
Battalion to Korea, José Raquel volunteers. Despite the opposition of
the two socially conscious family members, La Cotena and Máximo, he
prefers to fight in a war abroad rather than participate in a social war
that directly affects him and the people of Colombia.

In the second section of the work, "El botín" (The booty), José Raquel
returns to Chambacú after the war with what he considers tangible evidence of his having triumphed over the oppression of Chambacú. He
glides into the ghetto on his sparkling motorcycle clutched by a Nordic
trophy-wife. These represent the booty of his experience. However, his
hero's welcome falls short of expectations. The people are more interested in his mode of transportation and his passenger than they are in
the driver. For her part, La Cotena is outraged and embarrassed by her
son's decision to bring a white Swedish woman to Chambacú: "'A white
woman?' She thought to herself again. 'What in the world could he
have been smoking that would make that fool bring a white woman to
Chambacú? Could she be a prostitute? Only God knows in what whore-
house he found her!'" ("'¿Una gringa?' Recapacitó. '¿Qué humos se
han metido en la cabeza de ese imbécil para traer una gringa a
Chambacú? ¿Será una puta? ¡Sabe Dios en qué burdel la recogió!'"
Chambacú, 92) La Cotena's attitude toward Inge, her wayward son's chosen life partner, reflects the distance José Raquel has placed between
himself and his people. La Cotena's speculation about Inge's social status
and about where José Raquel might have met her underscores La
Cotena's image of Chambacú and its marginalization. As a "gringa,"
Inge has no place in their oppressed and downtrodden society. The fact
that her son feels comfortable enough to expose Inge to the conditions
of Chambacú persuades La Cotena that Inge must be a woman of ill
repute, one well acquainted with such conditions. The fact is that Inge's
arrival in Chambacú has more to do with José Raquel than with her.
His main concern is elevated social standing through their union. His

12. Ibid., 54.

mindset embodies the concept of "blanquamiento," or "whitening," the process of attaching himself to the dominant, white structure. José is not interested in participating in social protest against those in power. Interestingly, while other members of the community gather outside the jail to protest his brother's wrongful imprisonment, José Raquel shows no concern.

In the concluding section of the work, José Raquel totally transcends community by becoming part of the establishment that continues to suppress the people of Chambacú. This "escapist" mentality of José Raquel culminates in his attempt to convince his wife to leave Chambacú:

> —Inge, I need you. Come with me. I want to take you out of this filth. We will go and live in Manga where we can forget about Chambacú. I'm a Sergeant now. I know that it ain't a lot of money, but I tell you secretly, they've promised me lots of money. We can live decently. I'll buy you dresses, a radio and . . . perhaps even a car. Go and get your things. You don't need to say good-bye.
>
> (—Inge, te necesito. Vengo por ti. Quiero sacarte de esta porquería. Nos iremos a vivir a Manga donde nunca sepamos nada de Chambacú. Ahora soy Sargento. Sé que no es mucho de sueldo, pero en secreto te digo que me han prometido muchos dólares. Viviremos decente-mente. Te compraré vestidos, radio y ... podía ser que hasta un automóvil. Entra y saca tus maletas. No necesitas despedir te.) (*Chambacú*, 215–16)

José Raquel desires to separate himself totally from the despair of Chambacú in order to live a "decent life," that of the rich whites who live in the neighboring town of Manga. He exhibits little to no desire to assist his fellow Chambacoans in their struggle to ameliorate their social situation. His solution is to retreat into the territory of the oppressor and assimilate into the "white," privileged world. He is an officer, with the rank of sergeant, and has totally disassociated himself from the toils and agonies of his people. Influenced by Captain Quirós, the representative of white, institutional oppression, José Raquel joins forces with the police in order to manipulate the Peace Corps for financial gain, using Chambacú as bait.

Colombian officials view José Raquel as the perfect means to exploit the altruism of the United States. He has allied himself with the authorities, thusly demonstrating his vulnerability to exploitation. Additionally, he is well acquainted with the poverty that exists in Chambacú.

Who is better able to exploit the poverty of Chambacú in order to argue for financial assistance from the American Peace Corps officials? This is a way of persecuting further the people of Chambacú. The government's true motives for gaining American philanthropic funding are to force the poor residents out and use their land to build a resort. The barbarous savages must be eliminated to allow civilization to prosper.

The novel ends with the violent death of Máximo during a demonstration against forces trying to gain control of Chambacú for the purpose of converting the island into a tourist location for Europeans and North Americans. Máximo's death represents the spirit of the revolution. Reminiscent of Domingo and *En Chimá*, the voice of social protest continues to resonate beyond the grave, inspiring the people to continue the struggle. As Marvin Lewis states:

> Máximo's death is not in vain because the seeds of rebellion have been sown and Chambacú inhabitants are prepared to fight against the soldiers and their corrupt officials . . . Máximo's speeches do have the ring of Black Power to them, and he is the catalyst for social action . . . Máximo is willing to take risks in order to improve the plight of his people.[13]

Máximo navigates the journey toward social equality for the Chambacoans. Like the invalid Domingo in *En Chimá* and Mamatoco in *La Calle 10*, Máximo emerges as the embodiment of hope. As a direct consequence of his efforts, black members of this displaced society mobilize themselves politically into one collective voice against racial inequity and second-class citizenship. Thus, *Chambacú* becomes the first novelistic attempt by Afro-Colombian Manuel Zapata Olivella to focus all eyes on the social inequalities of black Colombians, thereby thematically "coloring," or "darkening," his literary production.

As in *En Chimá*, the concept of magical realism can be found in *Chambacú*. Underneath the surface of social protest, revolution, and violence lies a system of beliefs rooted in the culturally based rites, rituals, and superstitions of the natives. To date, no critic has explored in depth the element of magical realism in *Chambacú*. However, magic realism is a prominent theme in *Chambacú*. Bonifacio is the resident medicine man, witch doctor of Chambacú while Petronilla, his wife, is the local tarot card reader. They represent the abiding attachment of the local populace

13. Lewis, *Treading the Ebony Path*, 107.

to superstitious and magical realities. Desperate to know the where-abouts of her nephew José Raquel, Petronilla resorts to the reading of tarot cards to discover his fate:

> The wrinkles slithered across the forehead of Aunt Petronilla. The card game. They seemed different to her, unknown. Curled up, neck stretched out and lips trembling, she assumed a palpable life that had never existed in her everyday reality. Superstition and magic transmitted vitality to her. Satan, the demonic spirit of evil. The soul in Purgatory. The nails of Christ. The prayer to banish Lucifer. The ribs of a bat. The whiskers of a black cat clipped on a fiery night. The warm blood of a billy goat. Supernatural powers riding in the minds of blacks since the distant pits of slavery. She knew that Bonifacio received his powers one night on the mountain of Pope from the Devil himself. With the help of Saint Jude Thaddeus, he also diffused evil. Over there, shining at his back. The saint and the devil. The cards knew both good and evil. Nothing was hidden from them. He stretched out his finger and felt the weight of the dark forces that guided him. He shuttered in the midst of them, his finger-nail trembling. He fell upon one. Bonifacio stuck out his lips. His only foretooth, with pus coming from his gums, stuck out yellowed. His dark hand picked up the card and he showed it to Petronilla. Without noticing its many colors, he read its hidden message:
> Jack on horseback. Your nephew will go on a long trip . . . possibly with no return. They are after him. . . . He has many things hidden. He should give them up. Pray for him as much as you can and stop looking for him.

> (Las arrugas serpentearon en la fuente de la tía Pertonilla. El juego de los naipes. Le parecían otros, desconocidos. Acurrucada, alargado el cuello y los labios temblorosos, tomaban una vida palpable que jamás exhibía en su existencia diaria. La superstición y la magía le comunicaban vitali-dad. Belcebú. El Anima Sola. Los clavos de Cristos. La oración para ale-jar a Lucifer. Las costillas de murciélago. Los bigotes de gato negro, recortados en noche de celo. La sangre fresca de chivato. Poderes sobre-naturales que venían Cabagando la mente de los negros de foso lejano de la esclavitud. Sabía que Bonifacio recibió sus misterios una noche en cerro de la Popa, de las mismas manos del diablo. También neutralizaba el mal con la ayuda de San Judas Tadeo. Allí alumbrado, a su espalda. El santo y el demonio. Las cartas conocían el bien y el mal. Nadase les ocultaba. Estiró el dedo y sintió el peso de las fuerzas ocultas que lo guia-ban. Titubeó sobre ellas, la uña temblorosa. Cayó sobre una. Bonifacio estirólos labios. Su único incisivo, con piorrea, se asomó amarillento. Su mano oscura tomó la carta y la monstró a Petronilla. Sin ver su poli-cromía leyó el oculto mensaje:

—Sota a caballo. Tú sobrina emprenderá un largo viaje ... quizás sin retorno. Lo persiguen.... Tiene escondidas muchas cosas. Debe entregarlas. Reza por él cuando puedas y deja de buscarlo.) (*Chambacú*, 52–53)

This extensive quote demonstrates the importance of magical realism in Zapata Olivella's novel. Bonifacio possesses black magic, conferred on him by the devil. Faith and belief, two major components of magic realism, merge as Petronilla displays her undoubting confidence in his supernatural powers. Petronilla is not the only villager who believes in Bonifacio's magic. The narrator indicates that other blacks both have and believe in these supernatural powers that are residuals or reminders of the Old World.

La Calle 10, *En Chimá*, and *Chambacú* represent the narrative advancement of Manuel Zapata Olivella's literary focus on Colombian hunger, violence, resistance, and hope. These themes form the literary parameters of the lives that unfold within the narrative texts. Noted in the analysis is the progressive "darkening" of his protagonists, emblematic of an unapologetic centering on the plight of Colombians of African ancestry.

Chapter IV

Manuel Zapata Olivella

The Postmodern Writer

Following the decade of skyrocketing popularity of Latin American fiction, the literary production of Manuel Zapata Olivella continued to flourish. From 1970 to 1980, he produced essays, short stories, plays, and novels. Continuing the representation of the African in Spanish America, Zapata Olivella allows the black narrative voice to loudly proclaim its existence and advances the literary leitmotifs of that cultural tradition. His three major works of the 1970s, "Tradición oral y conducta en Córdoba" (1972), *El hombre colombiano* (1974), and "El substrato psicoafectivo y recreador del negro en el castellano americano" (1978), reveal a strong Afro-Colombian presence.

During the 1980s, Zapata Olivella published two volumes of essays: *Nuestra voz: Aportes del habla popular latinoamericano al idioma español* (1987) and *Las claves mágicas de América: raza, clase, cultura,* (1989). Two of his works published in the 1940s, *Tierra* and *He visto* were reprinted. He also published *Changó* and *El fusilamiento del diablo.*

With *Changó,* Olivella engages in an exploration of postmodernist discourse from the standpoint of the African diaspora. Metafiction becomes a predominant strategy. In assessing the impact on this innovation, Linda Hutcheon's work on postmodernity serves as the theoretical framework. In addition, the critical insights of Raymond Williams provide substantive clarifications.

Linda Hutcheon offers a useful and encompassing definition that has generally been regarded as a concise explanation of the complex topic of postmodernism:

> Postmodernism is a period label generally given to cultural norms since the 1960s that display certain characteristics such as reflexivity, irony and a mixing of popular and high art forms. . . . Postmodern literature has been called a literature of replenishment (Barth), on the one hand, and the literature of an inflationary economy (Newman), on the other. In

short, there is little agreement on the reasons for its existence or on the evaluation of its effects.[1]

This explanation presents a broad spectrum for the application of post-modernism by virtue of there being definitive explanation as to what it is, or why it exists. Hutcheon initiates her explanatory discourse on post-modernism by pointing to the origin of other theories later transplanted to literary analysis. She then situates the postmodernist approach to literature between two polar thoughts or philosophies: those of John Barth and Charles Newman. In addition, Hutcheon identifies common denominators used to define postmodernism. In terms of literature, these common characteristics include self-consciousness, historiographic metafiction, irony, parody, and subversion. In her *Poetics of Postmodernism*, she also links postmodernist thought to the epistemological ideologies of capitalism, patriarchy, imperialism, Marxism, feminism, poststructural-ism, and postcolonialism. Hutcheon points out the convoluted, contra-dictory nature of this term, which is essentially the articulation of that which it seeks to destroy:

> Of all the terms bandied about in both current cultural theory and con-temporary writing on the arts, postmodernism must be the most over- and under-defined. It is usually accompanied by a grand flourish of neg-ativized rhetoric: we hear of discontinuity, disruption, dislocation, de-centering, indeterminacy, and antitotalization. What all these words literally do (precisely by their disavowing prefixes—dis, de, in, anti) is in-corporate that which they aim to contest.[2]

Hutcheon recognizes that it represents an almost total inconsistency. She states further that postmodern is "fundamentally contradictory, res-olutely historical, and inescapably political."[3] She views postmodernism as a "rethinking of history" in terms of the representation of a singular truth arguing that therein lies implicit "truths."

As has been noted, placing Latin American literary production within the confines of a movement with defined chronological limit is problematic. Literature constitutes a continuum from one movement to the next. Major characteristics from a preceding movement are fused

1. Linda Hutcheon in *Encyclopedia of Contemporary Literary Theory*, 612.
2. Linda Hutcheon, *The Poetics of Postmodernism: History, Theory, Fiction* (New York: Routledge, 1988), 3.
3. Ibid., 4.

with innovations of the one that follows. As an example, early Latin American modernism was influenced by and continues to use some of the aesthetic practices of Latin American romanticism. The initial poetic works of Mexican Manuel Gutiérrez Nájera offer a case in point. Additionally, leitmotifs of Spanish American romanticism such as the conflict between civilization and barbarism infiltrated Latin American modernist fiction. The same holds true for postmodernism in Latin America. A vast majority of literary critics cite the close of the Boom decade as the beginning of postmodernist fiction in Spanish America. However, some critics and scholars are still skeptical regarding postmodernism in Latin American literature and question its applicability. Doris Sommer and George Yudice are two such scholars. In a coauthored article they argue that postmodernism and Latin American literature are incompatible:

> Latin American literature, then, does not fit comfortably into the category of postmodernism. On the one hand, it shares the postmodernist concern for the marginal, an ambiguous concept that has economic, sociological, and literary meaning. On the other, it is too concerned with its own identity to serve as a sheer surface on which a hegemonic postmodern culture mirrors itself.[4]

In the article, the authors refer to the decline in literary production during the 1970s and 1980s, and to concerns of identity formation within that cultural context. Nevertheless, it can be argued that in the 1970s and 1980s, many Latin American countries—Argentina, for example— had a recognized national body of literature that established a cultural and national identity, a fact which undermines Sommer and Yudice's arguments. If the proposed date for the inception of postmodernist thought in Latin American literature had been the 1940s and 1950s, their conclusion would have more credibility. Still, it is incontestable that Latin American literature is both unique and problematic. Its endemic reliance upon historical truths to project a fictional representation of a cultural reality renders it distinct in literary analysis. Postmodern Latin American literature projects the historical reality of the people as they adjust to the complexities that are unique to their regions and nations,

---

4. Doris Sommer and George Yudice, "Latin American Literature from the 'Boom' On," in *Postmodern Fiction: A Bio-Bibliographical Guide*, ed. Larry McCaffery (New York: Greenwood, 1986), 199.

and encompasses an engagement of many ideologies such as Marxism, feminism, capitalism, and imperialism. Many writers have ventured beyond the borders of their geographical confines in search of their "space" within the larger community using many ideologies and strategies.

The literary critic Leslie Fiedler introduced this "new" concept of postmodernism to academic circles of the United States in the 1970s. Although widely viewed as a phenomenon of the 1970s, many literary historians actually record the initial usage of postmodernism just after the Second World War. Interestingly, Raymond Williams indicates that some twenty-five years after introducing the term, Fiedler expressed regret for ever using the term due to the convoluted and misappropriated meanings that had become attached to it.

Postmodernism soon became the novelty "-ism" as North American and European scholars, artists, and intellectuals embraced the evolving movement of the epoch. However, in the context of Latin America, postmodernism did not enter intellectual jargon until the 1980s. Moreover, this entrée was not via Fiedler and the United States. Rather, for Latin America, Europe provided the influence as it had in the past. Europe has always been the impetus for intellectual and cultural movements in the arts and literature, in particular the cultural mecca of Paris. Latin American literary figures have been fascinated by Paris since the early nineteenth century. Consequently, the debate generated by a critical essay entitled "The Postmodern Condition" by French scholar Jean-François Lyotard spread rapidly to Latin America intellectuals. However, literary critics continue to look to Hutcheon as a leading authority on postmodernism in literary criticism.

One of Hutcheon's theoretical components of postmodernism does apply to Zapata Olivella's *Changó:* that of historiographic metafiction. For Hutcheon, historiographic metafictional novels are:

> both intensely self-reflexive and yet paradoxical also lay claim to historical events and personages. . . . Historiographic metafiction incorporates all three of these domains: that is, its theoretical self-awareness of history and fiction as human constructs (historiographic metafiction) is made the grounds for its rethinking of the forms and content of the past.[5]

Hutcheon reminds us that before the rise of scientific history in the late nineteenth century, literature and history were considered "branches

5. Hutcheon, *Poetics of Postmodernism,* 5.

from the same tree of learning" for the purpose of interpreting experience. Later, the two disciplines were viewed as mutually exclusive, an exclusivity that postmodern theory seeks to challenge. In assessing the commonalities between literature and history, Hutcheon reveals that the two disciplines can coexist:

> They have both been seen to derive their force more from verisimilitude than from any objective truth; they are both identified as linguistic constructs, highly conventionalized in their narrative forms, and not at all transparent either in terms of language or structure; and they appear to be equally intertextual, deploying the texts of the past within their own complex textuality.[6]

Ten years after the publication of *A Poetics of Postmodernism*, Raymond Williams, in his *Postmodernidades Latinoamericanas* (1998), deals with the issue of postmodernity in Latin America, focusing on postmodern literary development in five South American nations: Colombia, Venezuela, Ecuador, Perú, and Bolivia. As a basis for his analysis, Williams focuses initially on the polemic of postmodernity in Latin America. In "Postmodernidad y América Latina" (Postmodernity and Latin America), he begins by providing background on the appearance of postmodernism and postmodernity in the Latin American vernacular. In the last ten years, a heated debate concerning postmodernity in Latin America has emerged. This debate centers on whether or not Latin America itself had fully reached modernity due to the postmodernist movement. Williams believes the doubts and indecision relative to this question have become less relevant in light of the term's societal context and its present-day colloquial usage:

> Nowadays, the words "postmodernity" and "postmodernism" already form part of the popular vocabulary of the Hispanic world, where not only specialty magazines publish academic essays about the theme, but also weekly political and fashion magazines are apt to refer to a "postmodern situation," "postmodern clothing" as elements of the times.[7]

Williams believes that the widespread acceptance of these two terms indicates the presence of postmodernity and lays to rest the question as to

6. Ibid., 105.
7. Raymond L. Williams, *Postmodernidades Latinoamericanas* (Bogotá: Fundacíon Universidad Central, 1998), 17.

whether or not Latin America is a part of the postmodern age. He makes the claim that authors like García Márquez in *Cien años de soledad* were instrumental in constructing literary realities that questioned truthful claims and actual experiences and can therefore be classified amongst the other postmodern writers. Although he does not include the works of Manuel Zapata Olivella in his study, *Chambacú* is another "modernist" text that was instrumental in constructing the literary reality of blacks in Latin America. As Williams mentions later in the study, such "truths" and "realities" predate the 1960s. They were in fact challenged in the 1940s in the work of Borges and other Spanish American writers. The essence of Williams's argumentative development relating to truths and nontruths in literature strikes at the core of literary postmodernism as described by Linda Hutcheon:

> Hutcheon proposes that the term postmodern novel is reserved for what she identifies as historiographic metafiction. This postmodern narrative, as the one that she describes, is drawn to call attention to the problematic of writing history, inviting itself to question the cognitive status of historical knowledge. Historiographic metafiction suggests that "truth" and "falsity" to the greater extent are not correct terms; instead, we should speak of truths in plurality.[8]

In essence, the entire exercise of writing fiction "laced" with historical references is one of the major tenets of postmodern literature. Historical writing represents one "truth" among many; historical literature, too, can reveal a number of "truths" within the confines of the bound pages.

The fourth chapter of Williams's study is devoted to the analysis of postmodernism in Colombia. Again, his focus is modernist literature produced in Colombia in the 1940s and 1950s, dates which he believes established the beginning of modernist fiction and a prelude to postmodernist fiction. Citing authors of the 1940s such as Tomás Vargas Osorio, Rafael Gómez Picón, and Jaime Ibáñez, Williams states that their intent was to publish fiction that was perceived as "modern." He believes that although their works contain elements viewed as modernist, they represent only the initial stages of modernist fiction in Colombia. Williams places the apogee of modernist fiction in the 1950s and 1960s with the publication of three major works: García Márquez's *La hojarasca*

8. Ibid., 34.

(1955), Alvaro Cepeda Samudio's *La casa grande* (1962), and Héctor Rojas Herazo's *Respirando el verano* (1962).

In his concluding comments on postmodernism in Colombian literature, Williams concurs with other critics of Spanish American literature that the modernist movement reached its peak in the 1960s with the Boom in Latin America. He, like other scholars, regards Gabriel García Márquez's *Cien años de soledad* as the quintessential postmodern work in both Colombian and Latin American literature.

Of all Zapata Olivella's works, *Changó,* in light of its intricate postmodern narrative structure is receiving the most critical attention from literary critics and scholars. For many, this is Zapata Olivella's "obra maestra." An overwhelming majority of critics also view *Changó* as the culmination of Zapata Olivella's discourse on the African diaspora. Consuming over twenty years of the author's creative effort, this novel emerges as a mythological construction of the African diaspora in the Americas and beyond. The major thread that unites all of its novelistic sections is Africa and the Yoruba religious tradition.

As a point of departure, it is important to understand the significance of the figure of Changó, the divine being whom the author uses to unify the novel. The African deity Changó, also spelled Xangó or Sangó, is the son of Yemayá and Orungán. Orungán gave birth to fourteen of the most important gods of Yoruba. As an addendum to the work itself, Zapata Olivella provides a lengthy "cuaderno de bitácora" (binnacle notebook) that serves as a compass for navigating the text's mythology. Within this notebook, the author provides a succinct description of the deity Changó and notes his position within the Yoruba faith:

> In the Yoruba mythology, he is the son of Yemaya and Orungán. He was the third sovereign ruler of the imperial state of Oyo, whose capital, Ife, situated in the vicinity of the Niger, was the birthplace of the Orichas, creators of the world. The life and adventures of Changó are enmeshed in African and American mythology where he is revered as the god of war, fertility and dance. In the syncretization with Catholic saints, he is identified as Saint Barbara.

> (En la mitología yoruba, hijo de Yemayá and Orungán. Fue el tercer soberano del estado imperial de Oyo, cuyo capital, Ife, ubicada en las cercanías del Níger, fue cuna de los Orichas creadores del mundo. La vida y hazañas de Changó se confunden en la mitología de Africa y América donde se le venera como al Dios de la guerra, la fecundidad y la

danza. En la sincretización con los santos católicos se le identifica con Santa Bárbara.) (*Changó*, 735)

Structurally, this work of over seven hundred pages is divided into five parts. The novel begins with a poetic verse that, in the style of an epic poem, offers an Afrocentric account of the creation of the world. The author utilizes mythological folklore, elements of history, interior monologue, dialogue, stream-of-consciousness, and fictional narration in order to advance the plot. The novel is set in Africa, where the author deals with the origin of the world from the point of view of the African deities.

Subsequent sections of the novel deal with issues confronting those Africans who were taken from the continent and dispersed throughout the Americas. Consequently, the novel serves as the fictional representation of the predicament of Afro-Americans in the diaspora.[9]

The section entitled "El Muntu Americano" (The American muntu), chronicles the struggles of Africans in a Colombian context. "La rebelión de los vodus" (The voodoo rebellion), the third part, is the fictional account of the conflicts of Africans in Haiti. The fourth part, "Las sangres encontradas" (Opposing bloods), deals with the involvement of Africans in the revolutionary movements in South America and Mexico. The final part of the novel, "Los ancestros combatientes" (Dueling ancestors), recounts the struggles for freedom and equality in North America.

In the introduction, Zapata Olivella informs the reader of the mission of Changó. The narration explains that the spirit of the African deity Changó, who was exiled as a result of having fallen from grace, seeks his revenge by condemning the people to slavery as punishment. The mythic elements of the story regarding enslavement recalls biblical tales such as Satan's reign on earth and the curse of Ham. Additionally, in the mode of a creationist text, this first section portrays sin as a result of man's inhumanity against man. Changó, like Satan, is expelled from paradise, and as a result, he wreaks havoc on the world.

The concept of *mestizaje* is an endemic one in *Changó*. The author's introductory comments immerse the reader in a world of cultural and biological mixing. Zapata Olivella begins this five-century voyage by

---

9. The use of Afro-American in this study connotes an inclusive representation of blacks in the Americas.

dealing first with the etiology of the title and its implication. The title is a compilation of two distinct cultural ideologies. *Changó* represents the mythological Yoruba god; *el gran Putas* is borrowed from a compilation of denotative and connotative images and from Colombian folklore forming *gran Putas*.[10] From the outset, the reader is made aware of the Afro-American reality in Latin America, the Caribbean, and North America.

In *Changó*, Zapata Olivella tries to unite the struggles of blacks in the African diaspora as they seek to gain liberation and to recover their identity. Probably one of the most profound summations of the novel comes from Marvin Lewis in *Treading the Ebony Path*. Lewis views this work as the *"total* novel of the Afro-American diaspora [emphasis mine]." This work is the first of its kind in Latin America in that it focuses on the plight of Africans in the Americas from their removal from Africa, through slavery and colonization to the Civil Rights era. Largely due to its comprehensiveness, the novel emerges, as Lewis suggests, as the "total novel of the Afro-American diaspora" in North, Central, and South America.[11]

A key element in *Changó* is the author's manipulation of time. Within the text, centuries of history are fictionally fused as the author unites the past with the present. Common throughout the entirety of the work is a dialogue among Agne Brown, who some critics say is a fictional representation of Angela Davis, and many black historical figures such as Toussaint L'Ouverture, Nat Turner, and Malcolm X. These interactions of the present and the past serve to create a continuum in the struggle of blacks in the diaspora as they progress from slavery to the present time. The underlying message is that the struggle against the oppressive hegemony of La Loba Blanca continues into the present.[12]

This continuum of time is crucial to the development and understanding of the text. As John Mbiti so states, the concept of time in African cosmology is connotatively and denotatively distinct from that of Westerners. Often, there is no separation between past, present, and future, which constitute a singular concept in the cycle of life. Clearly Zapata Olivella utilizes this Africanized concept of time in *Changó* as characters

10. For readers interested in the author's explication of the construction of "el gran Putas," please consult the fourth footnote of the novel's introduction.

11. Lewis, *Treading the Ebony Path*, 118.

12. Within the text, the author uses "La Loba Blanca" as a symbolic metaphor for the dominant white mass.

appear anachronistically and do not adhere to the expectations of Western readers. Instead, the author presents interplay between diachronic and synchronic time. Notes Marvin Lewis: "In *Changó, the Great SOB* there is a movement from *synchrony*, or mythic and cyclic time, toward *diachrony*, history in which time is seen as a linear sequence."[13] This shift towards diachrony, to which Lewis alludes, reveals a postmodern unconventionality. That which Lewis sees as "diachrony" is the narrative subversion of synchrony for the purpose of novelistic contextualization. By constructing this work within the framework of Africanicity, Olivella rejects certain hegemonic constructs and "liberates" his writing from Westernized conventions (such as time).

Many of Manuel Zapata Olivella's works use historical realities. From his first published work to his last, the sociopolitical and literary "realities" that exist within Latin America and other parts of the world are brought to light. However, *Changó* is the text that most warrants a postmodern analysis in this regard. *Changó* embraces the antithetical objectives of postmodern literature in that it decenters, displaces, and fictionalizes conventional historical accounts of Africans in the Americas. Yvonne Captain-Hidalgo affirms that this novel is "the first successful novel of the African diaspora in the Americas," contrasting Zapata Olivella with eighteenth-century African American writers such as Phyllis Wheatley and Jupiter Hammon, who also explored the trope of Africanicity in literature. However, despite her favorable appraisal of the work, Captain-Hidalgo argues that the novel is virtually plotless: "Basically, *Shango* is a plotless 'tale' that through a type of extended, narrative iteration manages to repeat in an engaging fashion the attempts of a people to win their freedom."[14] The plot, I would argue, centers on the ever-continuous striving of diasporic Africans to achieve freedom and liberation from racial oppression.

In the spirit of postmodernism, Zapata Olivella "decenters" the narrative structure of the work and "Africanizes" his narrative approach. It is indisputable that within the Africana literary tradition, narrative repetition is mimetic of, and directly akin to, literary oral tradition.[15] Repetition and orality are commonly associated with the Africana literature. It is precisely through this approach that the novel earns its reputation

13. Lewis, *Treading the Ebony Path*, 113.
14. Captain-Hidalgo, *Culture of Fiction*, 152, 154.
15. *Africana literary tradition* is a term that scholars and critics have begun to use in reference to literature of the African diaspora.

as the best representation of a work on the African diaspora, an observation made by many leading Africana literary critics. Ian Smart suggests that Zapata Olivella is trying to evoke the idea of liberationist literature: "Zapata's creative intention is quite clear: his novel is meant to construct an African mythological framework that will explicate not merely his fictional universe but, more pertinently, the real world."[16] Smart clearly delineates a major focus of Hutcheon's definition of historiographic metafiction: the blending of fiction and reality. He notes that the work is "self-consciously liberationist." Smart acquires corroboration for his claim from Marvin Lewis in *Treading the Ebony Path*. For Lewis, a major "thematic preoccupation" of the literary aesthetic of Manuel Zapata Olivella is that of liberation: social, political, and economic.

In spite of *Changó's* fictionalized representation of the black experience in South America, Haiti, and the United States, the major emphasis of this study will focus on the last section of the work, which introduces the author's preoccupation with the diaspora outside of Latin America. In "Los ancestros combatientes," the geographical locale shifts from Latin America to North America. The metafictional quality presented in this section of the novel is that of the North American diaspora and the infusion of black North American historical figures and events within the narrative context of a fictional representation.

The four preceding sections of the novel explore the concept of diaspora in the context of colonial Latin America and Haiti and are vital to the work's developmental movement. Furthermore, they set the tone for how this author interplays fiction and history in this work. Ian Smart underscores the significance of all the sections of the novel: "They present in accurate historical sequence the focal points of the drama of the African-ancestored Americans' experience in the New World."[17]

These first four sections present the initial interaction and confrontation among Africans, Indians, and Spaniards as cultural traditions are placed into direct confrontation. The major historical occurrences referred to in the second section are slavery in Colombia and colonialism. Two important historical figures emerge as principal characters: Benkos Biojo and Father Claver. Through Benkos Biojo, Zapata Olivella de-

---

16. Ian Isidore Smart, *Amazing Connections: Kemet to Hispanophone Africana Literature* (Washington, D.C.: Original World Press, 1996), 115.
17. Ibid., 128.

picts Colombian slavery and the efforts of slaves to resist by establishing a *palenque,* a maroon society of runaway slaves, at San Basilio. Biojo orchestrates the plan near Cartagena de Indias. The Inquisition is presented in the narrative as a means to convert Africans. The historical figure Father Pedro Claver, a Spanish Jesuit priest, becomes a chronicler of the atrocities of colonial slavery in Colombia and an advocate for the slaves in Cartagena.

The history of a slave revolt in the Americas is also detailed in the text. The revolution in Haiti is depicted in the third section of the work. The fourth section emphasizes the historical period of Latin American independence through the characters Simón Bolívar, the liberator of Colombia and other Latin American countries from Spanish colonial rule, Prudencio Padillo, a hero in both Colombian and Venezuelan independence, and José María Morales, hero of the Mexican Revolution. The fifth part of the novel, the section of most interest for this study, explores the history of the African diaspora in North America. Zapata Olivella continues his use of mythological folklore with the introduction of the messenger of Changó, Ngafúa, who is sent to give orders to the fictional Agne Brown. Much like the Virgin Mary, King David, Solomon, and other biblical figures, Agne Brown is chosen by Changó to carry out his mission in North America. Olivella employs flashback, which allows the spirit of Changó to chronicle the history of Africans in the United States, beginning with slavery. These encounters with historical ancestors equip Agne for her task.

The first order is that she return to the period of North American slavery in order to reassess the connotative stigma ascribed to it. She is instructed by the gods to not view this epoch of history with shame, but to embrace the strength and fortitude of the people who, despite the horrific experiences of that institution, remained steadfast and survived:

> You don't have to be shamed by slavery of the past! The people emerge strong, strengthened of all their pains. Look for your trench in the ashes of your ancestors. You are the experience of those who follow you, awaited you and will accompany you in the cold night of your slum quarter.
>
> (¡Que el pasado de esclavitud no tenga por qué avergonzarlos! El Muntu surge valiente, fortalecido de todas sus heridas. Busca tu trinchera en las cenizas de tus huesos. Experiencia eres de aquéllos que te siguen, te esperaron y acompañarán en la fría noche de los tugurios.) (*Changó,* 501)

Agne is advised to gain strength from the African and African American ancestors of the past as she experiences the plight of Africans in the United States. As she prepares for the journey, Agne is told to breathe the fresh air of the beginning of her new life, to forget the brand that white people put on her soul. This new life is one that is defined by liberationist ideology. She is instructed to break the oppressive forces within, which the institution of slavery has imprisoned her soul. She soon realizes that to acquire the freedom proposed within the text, she must liberate herself from the crippling negative memories of her past. On her historical journey, the present meets the past, and the two unite in order to create an unbroken timeline.

As Agne historicizes the plight of enslaved Africans, the reader is introduced to "el flaco Harry" (skinny Harry) and "el rechoncho Jones" (fat Jones). These fictional characters are imbued with historical significance: they represent white slave masters and overseers. The victim is Agne's "father." While affixing "father" with the prefix "fore" would be most appropriate, Agne, in referring to her *padre* in the work, indicates not a personal identification, but one that has a broader scope. The interaction between the symbolic representations of father, forefathers, and ancestors creates an epic sense of collectivity:

> But when this happened, when the rope was placed around my father's neck and the other three men pulled from the other end and the heavy body of my father rises until his head touches the ceiling, the fat Mr. Jones will have already rested the nose of the shotgun on his face. I sank my hands in the ground behind the cherry trees and none the less, now I know that I saw everything. Next to him is skinny Jones who my father would always help as the rheumatic pains upon cutting in the woods hound him.

> (Pero cuando esto aconteció, cuando le pone la soga al cuello y los otros tres hombres tiraron de la otra punta y el pesado cuerpo de mi padre sube hasta tocar con su cabeza el techo, ya el rechoncho Jones le habrá apoyado la punta de la escopeta en la cara. Yo hundía las manos en la tierra detrás de los cerezos y sin embargo, ahora sé que lo vi todo. Junto a él está el flaco Jones a quien mi padre socorrerá siempre que lo acosen los dolores reumáticos al hachar en el bosque.) (*Changó*, 503)

This quote, focusing on a singular event, is emblematic of the experience of a collective whole and solidifies the notion of Africanized time as a continuous present. Agne retells an emasculating incident that was not uncommon during slavery and its aftermath in the United States. Her father and other Africans are harnessed with rope around their necks, as if they were cattle desiring to flee the clutches of an oppressive shepherd, and are to be lynched. She remembers in minute detail the events that surround this occurrence that leaves her orphaned. The lynching of Timothy Brown reflects a historical reality in the lives of untold numbers of black men. Conversely, Agne becomes the symbol of all those left orphaned as a result of such heinous actions. Sadly, Agne learns that the same harness is metaphorically present in twentieth-century society through the oppressive control of black Americans by the dominant white culture.

One of the most metatextual strategies in the text is the author's use of historical figures, events, and narrations within a fictional context. Although the narrative voice does not recount historicized events in the chronological style of historical discourse, their inclusion serves as a reminder of history as Agne Brown meanders through time in search of understanding. After the realities of slavery and lynching are disclosed, the narrative voice continues to present people and events taken from African American history in the United States:

> Agne Brown, in order for you to value the positive or the terrible of my work it is necessary that your visit extends into the depth of time. That way, you will distinguish the African Daniel Hale Williams preparing himself to repeat the great achievement only before achieved by the great surgeons of ancient Egypt: opening and suturing the heart of a live patient. You will see in the old Tuskegee Institute Professor George Washington Carver nourishing the roots of coffee trees with synthetic sap. Listen well! The young Granville Woods transmits the first wireless signal from a moving train.

> (Agne Brown, para valorar lo positivo o nefasto de mi obra es necessario que tu visita se extiende en la profundidad del tiempo. Así podrás distinguir al ekobio Daniel Hale Williams disponiéndose a repetir la hazaña sólo antes lograda por los cirujanos del antiguo Egipto: abrir y suturar el corazón de un paciente vivo. Verás en el viejo Instituto en Tuskegee al profesor George Washington Carver alimentando con savia sintética las raíses de los cafetos. ¡Oye! El joven Granville Woods transmite la primera señal inalámbrica desde un tren en movimiento.) (*Changó*, 537)

This quote situates the text in the metafictional mode in several ways. First, there is the mixture of fictional characters and actual historical personalities such as Daniel Hale Williams, George Washington Carver and Granville Williams. Ngafúa, a fictional construct, instructs Agne about historical truths relative to the contributions of African Americans in North America. It is from these ancestors that the fictional character Agne Brown finds strength and gains respect for blacks of the North American diaspora. This knowledge serves as the foundation for the forthcoming liberationist revolutions of the 1960s, presented within the text through references to the urban riots, Martin Luther King, the Civil Rights Movement, Malcolm X, and the Nation of Islam.

The text also reconstructs the conventional power paradigm through European decentering, a strategy noted by African American scholar Cornel West: "The current 'postmodern' debate is first and foremost a production of significant First World reflections upon the centering of Europe that take such forms as the demythification of European cultural predominance and the deconstruction of European philosophical edifices."[18] In his essay, West assesses the impact black American culture has had on North American and world culture in the second half of the twentieth century. He concludes that the impact of black culture on North American society has displaced the predominance of European influence. In the text, Africa is placed in the power-playing arena of dominant cultures due to the technological, educational, and medical advances of blacks in the United States.

The text makes a pivotal observation relative to the "demythification of European cultural predominance and the deconstruction of European philosophical edifices" by indicating that Hale Williams repeated successfully a medical procedure that had previously been performed only in the ancient African culture of Egypt. Thus, Egypt is projected as the birthplace of a procedure that revolutionized modern medicine. Whereas Europe has been positioned traditionally as the world leader in the field of medicine, Zapata Olivella demystifies this worldview by promoting an Afrocentric view of history.

A final metatextual strategy is the manipulation and subversion of the Western concept of time. An interesting observation made by Lucía Ortiz is that historiography can be disrupted by bringing historical dates and figures into the narrative present, thus dislodging linear chronology

18. Cornel West, "Black Culture and Postmodernism," reprinted in *A Postmodern Reader,* ed. Joseph Natoli and Linda Hutcheon (Albany: State University of New York Press, 1993), 391.

in narrative discourse: "Narrative temporality is manifested directly by juxtaposing the past and the future in the same phrase and the African concept of the Universe is established as the conductive thread that disrupts the linear system of time in the dominant Western culture."[19]

Borrowing from John Mbiti's explanation of the African concept of the universe, Ortiz postulates that the universe represents a continuation of the past and future. However, more in light with Mbiti's definition, this temporal projection of the universe is one that embraces in a single continuum all three divisions of time: past, present, and future. Ortiz is correct in her assertion that in *Changó*, Zapata Olivella presents a juxtaposition of the past and future. However, this juxtaposition includes the present as well. The past and the future are manifestations of a continuous present. Throughout the work, the lines of temporal demarcation intersect with one another and are rendered void of chronological precision. Narrative strategies of such and others mentioned in this analysis of *Changó* offer textual support for the argument that this work characteristically emerges as a postmodern novel.

19. Lucía Ortiz, *La novela colombiana hacia finales del siglo veinte* (New York: Peter Lang, 1997), 61. All translations are my own.

Chapter V

An Exploration of Postcolonial Tri-ethnicity in
Levántate mulato, Las claves mágicas de América, and *Changó, el gran putas*

If one were to summarize the leitmotifs that permeated the literary discourse of Manuel Zapata Olivella from the late 1980s into the 1990s, the author's preoccupation with racial/ethnic identity would surface as a dominant example. This Colombian writer of mixed ethnic background journeys toward self-identification and self-celebration in three works: *Levántate, Las claves,* and *Changó*. These pivotal works represent a trilogy of racial/ethnic consciousness encompassing Spanish, African, and Indian heritage. His journey toward ethnic identification facilitates a better understanding of "race" as it is understood in Latin America and in the world.

Levántate depicts the author's coming to terms with his personal racial identity. A major focus of the work is the author's acceptance, identification, and celebration of his African heritage. *Levántate* is the first work in the trilogy exploring the concept of tri-ethnicity. In *Las claves,* the author adds another dimension to the racial triad of Latin America. With a firm understanding of his Spanish and African ancestry, Zapata Olivella proclaims the need for postcolonial Spanish Americans to fully embrace all aspects of their heritage. It is within this series of essays that the author embraces the tri-ethnic composition of Latin America. The final work of the trilogy on race and ethnicity is *Changó*. *Changó* is the author's most ambitious literary work to date fictionalizing the history of the African diaspora. *Changó* represents the third dimension of the author's construction of ethnic identity. The point of departure for this analysis of tri-ethnicity is the creation of the multiracial/ethnic subject, which is the direct result of colonialism and the institution of slavery in the New World. An appreciation of the author's construct of racial identity requires a definition of postcoloniality and an explanation of its intersection with postmodernist thought.

Postmodern theory, because of its emphasis on ideological factors (such as imperialism), intersects with many other contemporary critical theories, one of which is postcolonialism. In its purest sense, the term applies chronologically to the epoch that immediately followed the abolition of colonial rule. In Latin America, this time frame would begin with the nineteenth century. However, the issue becomes problematic when critics and scholars try to limit its application to literary works produced only during this period. Consequently, literary critics since the 1970s have broadened the scope of this terminology to encompass the myriad of experiences in societies that were formerly European colonies. The term *postcolonial* today has to do with the political, social, and economic institutions of former imperial colonies and the psychological ramifications for its subjects that are the result of colonial rule. The *Encyclopedia of Contemporary Literary Theory* offers the following definition:

> Post-Colonial theory is a term for a collection of theoretical and political strategies used to examine culture (literature, politics, history and so forth) of former colonies of the European empires, and their relationship to the rest of the world. While it embraces no single method or school, post-colonial theory—or, more accurately, theories—share many assumptions: they question the salutary effects of empire (visible in phrases such as "the gift of civilization," "the British literary heritage" or even "the Renaissance") and raise such issues as racism and exploitation.[1]

Colloquially speaking, postcoloniality refers to a "slave mentality," that is to say, a mindset that betrays the lingering psychological effects of hegemonic imperial control, due to either slavery or colonization. The impact of imperial control is so strong that the forces of oppression and subjugation continue to control the thought process of the oppressed even after liberation. Consequently, a lowered sense of self-esteem can be detected in those formerly colonized or enslaved.

In an attempt to expand the original concept, the editors of the *Post-Colonial Studies Reader* give a broader definition:

> Post-Colonial theory involves discussion about experience of various kinds: migration, slavery, suppression, resistance, representation, difference, race,

1. *Encyclopedia of Contemporary Literary Theory*, 155.

gender, place, and responses to the influential master discourses of imperial Europe such as history, philosophy and linguistics, and the funda-
mental experiences of speaking and writing by which all of these come
into being.[2]

The wider scope of this definition makes it more useful for this study.
The racialized self versus the "other," the non-Africanized subject (or
the subject lacking African heritage), is a central focus of the works examined in this chapter.

Postcolonial issues of race, ethnicity, exploitation, oppression, racism,
social struggle, resistance, and ethnic composition emerge as the predominant thematic focus in the works of Manuel Zapata Olivella. His
autobiography, *Levántate,* recounts his journey toward understanding his
African heritage and relates accounts of the author's family life, revela-
tions that reinforce his level of black consciousness. *Las claves* problema-
tizes issues pertaining to race, class, and culture in the Americas as
a result of colonization, racism, exploitation, and oppression. Zapata
Olivella's discourse on race and ethnicity culminates in his lengthy
Changó, wherein the issue of the African diaspora is cast in a global context. All these texts navigate the convoluted concept of race in the
Americas.

Defining "race" is not a simple task. This socially derived concept
varies based on the academic discipline that defines it. Social scientists
view race as a sociopolitical function that is manipulated for social and
political control. Biological scientists and geneticists view race as a biological entity. However, cultural anthropologists such as Franz Boas
have been instrumental in broadening the discourse on race by refut-
ing any correlation between race and genetic composition. In the hu-
manities, however, it is generally accepted that race is indeed a socially
engineered construct. Michael Omi and Howard Winant postulate
that the New World provides a possible point of departure for the race
debate:

> Race consciousness, and its articulation in theories of race, is largely a
> modern phenomenon. When European explorers in the New World
> "discovered" people who looked different from themselves, these "na-
> tives" challenged then the existing conceptions of the origins of human

2. Bill Ashcroft, Gareth Griffiths, and Helen Tiffin, *The Post-Colonial Studies
Reader* (London: Routledge, 1995), 2.

species, and raised disturbing questions as to whether *all* could be considered the same in the "family of man."[3]

Omi and Winant see the New World as the genesis of a discourse relating to "otherness" based on visual perceptions of physical and phenotypic differences. Furthermore, they view the encounters between different ethnicities as a religious dilemma for the European explorers who believed that God created only one species of man. History has recorded that by the time of the Conquest, Europeans had already encountered a second species of man, the African. In the New World they found a third species.

Slavery, servitude, and miscegenation are major foci of Manuel Zapata Olivella's works. He fully develops his construction of a postcolonial identity with his exploration of *mestizaje* in *Changó*. This work exposes the author's concept of tri-ethnicity, his view of the diaspora as a tripartite phenomenon. For Zapata Olivella, Africa is the central unifying element for the discovery of identity among people of the diaspora. The first chapter of this novel clearly sets the tone for the emergence of a multiethnic society with its genesis in Africa. An initial mythological epic poem encapsulates the African origin of the diaspora that was to evolve in the Americas and other geographical locations throughout the world. This "creationist" view in poetic form establishes the symbolic womb that gives birth to the multiethnic American:

> But America womb of the Indian, virgin womb raped seven times by the white man fertilized for the *Muntu* with your blood sweat and your screams—reveal to me Changó—a child will be born black son white son Indian son half earth half tree half wood half fire through himself redeemed.

> (Pero América matriz del indio, vientre virgen violado siete veces por la Loba fecundada por el Muntu con su sangre sudores y sus gritos—revelóme Changó—parirá un niño hijo negro hijo blanco hijo indio mitad tierra mitad árbol mitad leña mitad fuego por sí mismo redimido.) (*Changó*, 86–87)

The mighty African god and Ngafúa, his messenger, foresee the birth of a new American, one who is the product of miscegenation. They predict

---

3. Michael Omi and Howard Winant, "Racial Formations," in *Sources: Notable Selections in Race and Ethnicity*, ed. Adalberto Aguirre Jr. and David V. Baker (Guilford: McGraw-Hill, 1998), 3–13.

that the emergence of this "new American" will result from historical rapes dating from colonialism and the institution of slavery in the Americas. Changó relates how this "species" will rebel and escape the oppressive forces of the white power structure in order to redeem himself. The underlying message to the people, *el Muntu,* is that all people of African descent share historical experiences and a common identity. Throughout the novel, the narrative voice challenges the descendents of the *Muntu* in the Americas to accept and embrace the beauty and the complexity of their mixed heritage. This acknowledgment and acceptance of self will strengthen them as they rise up against *La Loba Blanca,* their white oppressor. After having established Africa as the common denominator, the author explores the diaspora in the context of colonial Latin America, Haiti, and the United States.

As Zapata Olivella expands his fictional representation in the three distinct geographical spaces of the African diaspora explored in the novel, the African origin of each establishes the point of departure. Thus, the chronological time frame in each section commences in the epoch of colonialism and slavery and advances to the postcolonial present. An identity is constructed that represents the postcolonial expression of people of African descent within a Hispanophone, Francophone, and Anglophone context. As the issue of identity is presented within the context of these language groupings, their etymological epistemology reveals the author's exploration of *mestizaje,* the emergence of beings that are biologically mixed. It is important to note that the author's concept of tri-ethnicity is not based solely on racial composition. It embraces the celebration of cultural syncretism as three distinct norms are conjoined to create a vastly unique entity. Hence, the appropriation of race by Zapata Olivella is from the standpoint of sociology; in that, race is perceived as a socially engineered construct for propagandistic purposes. The principal racial and cultural components for these mixed ethnicities come from Africa, Europe, and Indigenous America. This is an underlying message embedded within the text. As the varying narrative voices probe the development of this tripartite ethnicity, the message to the Muntu in *Changó* is that self-identification will lead to acceptance and liberation. Like the other protagonists in the novel, Agne Brown must journey through the Africana experience in North America in order to gain a sense of connection with her African ancestors, thereby better understanding and appreciating her identity. From this sojourn, she will gain the strength to celebrate herself as a part of the diaspora.

Agne revisits the horrors of North American slavery, the rape of women and the oppression of her people by the dominant white oligarchy, but she also relives the redemptive reality of resistance. In other sections of the work, racial and cultural mixing are seen as positive developments. Simón Bolívar, for example, is reminded of his mixed heritage: "It is the spirit of your black grandmother, reborn in you, more alive, stronger because the deceased are enriched with the experiences of the living." (—Es el alma de tu abuela negra, renacida en ti, más viva, más fuerte porque los difuntos se enriquecen con las experiencias de los vivos. *Changó*, 364) It is through these constant reminders that the spirit of Changó and his messengers communicate the need for racial identification and acceptance. The fictionalized character of Simón Bolívar is forced to acknowledge the truth of his mixed identity. The author fully presents his quest for racial clarification within the novel in order to fill in the gap of history. The fact that many historical accounts strip major figures of Latin American history of their Africanness compels this author to reveal a number of "truths" that have been deliberately overlooked. The search for postcolonial identity and identification becomes an avenue for self-acceptance, self-celebration, and liberation for many Latin Americans in this seminal work of fiction.

The second pivotal work of this trilogy dealing with Zapata Olivella's discourse on race/ethnicity in the Americas is the autobiographical *Levántate mulato: "Por mi raza hablará el espíritu."* Like the works of many other Latin American writers, *Levántate* was first published in Europe. The autobiography was translated into French and published as *Lève-toi, mulâtre* in Paris in 1987, where it was well received. It was awarded the prestigious Parisian New Human Rights Prize for Literature. In 1990, Rei Andes Limitada published the Spanish version in Bogotá as *Levántate*. Heralded as Zapata Olivella's primary autobiographical work, *Levántate* is much more than a mere autobiography. Its historical structure offers a succinct account of the indigenous inhabitants of the Caribbean prior to the arrival of the Europeans up to the twentieth century. It encompasses the arrival of Africans in the New World and slavery and its aftermath. Zapata Olivella's professional experience as an anthropologist resonates throughout the work as he discusses the physical and cultural origins, social customs, and beliefs of those living in the Americas. However, Zapata Olivella subverts the genre of the historical novel by incorporating autobiographical elements in his work. The narrative voice alternates between the first-person and the third-person, omniscient narrator. In consequence, Zapata Olivella manages to personalize history. The intimate accounts of his life serve as the narrative basis for the telling of a personal history shared by many.

The work comprises a prologue, an introduction, and ten chapters. The prologue "Zapata Olivella proclama el mestizaje" (Zapata Olivella proclaims miscegenation), written by the Colombian Morales Benítez, announces the general theme of the work. Benítez declares that *Levántate* offers a thorough exposition of miscegenation of the Ibero-American continent. As to its autobiographical nature and value, Morales Benítez believes that this work exceeds the literary limitations of pure autobiography:

> One could affirm that it is a volume in which the memories vibrate. It has a more transcendental mission. Apparently, one could think that it is an autobiography, in which pass references to diverse experiences, traces about legends, remembrances of readings in order to locate nuances of several cultures. That is not the single projection of his writing. It penetrates more shrewdly. Zapata Olivella wishes to jeopardize, in a continental understanding, all the racial tendencies that have some African vigor. (*Levántate*, 7–8)

Morales Benítez argues that one of the major motives of the work is to present a global perspective on Africanicity, not just a peripheral account of the life of Manuel Zapata Olivella. *Levántate* provides a definition of what it means to be Colombian, Latin American, and a part of the African diaspora in the Americas, an American of mixed-race and multiple ethnicities.

The introduction confirms the assertions of Otto Morales Benítez. Zapata Olivella begins his discourse on "race" and identity by probing his own culture, identity, "race," and destiny. The introduction is entitled, "¿Cuál es mi cultura, mi raza mi destino?" (What is my culture, my race, my destiny?), and the initial lines are an acknowledgment of the author's racial makeup and mixed ethnic identity:

> By the time that I was twenty years old, I was fully cognizant of my mixed ancestry. But this conviction triggered distressing answers. The terms mestizo, bastard, mulatto, zambo, so looked down upon in American history and society, were demanding of me a consistent attitude about myself, my blood and my ancestors.

> (Para entonces yo tenía veinte años y plena conciencia de mi hibridez. Pero este convencimiento me despertaba angustiosas respuestas. Los tér-

minos mestizo, bastardo, mulato, zambo, tan despreciados en la historia
y sociedad americanas, me reclamaban una actitud consecuente conmigo mismo, con mi sangre, con mis ancestros.) (*Levántate*, 17)

At the outset, Zapata Olivella introduces the major focus and greater
purpose of his autobiographical work: a pilgrimage toward self-discovery
and a definition of self. He takes note of the fact that the discourse of
race in the Americas, as articulated by scholars such as Víctor Raúl
Haya de la Torre, José Vasconcelos, and José Carlos Mariátequi, deals
primarily with the indigenous masses, while relegating the plight of the
African to a black hole of silence that is ever-present, but never fully explored or recognized. He states that "in their eagerness to vindicate the
Indian, they forget about the Negro" (Pero en su afán de reivindicar al
indio, ambos se olvidaron del negro. *Levántate*, 17).

Thus, *Levántate* serves as a rewriting of the history of the Americas,
an attempt to reinscribe what scholars and historians have refused to
acknowledge: the African component of the New World experience and
the presence of a global African diaspora. For Zapata Olivella, to deny
one all aspects of his multiracial heritage amounts to a form of normal-
ized eugenics that leads to self-hatred. He can fully understand himself
only by celebrating and acknowledging all that he is: Spanish, Indian,
and African.

Many North American scholars hail Zapata Olivella's efforts in this
work. Richard Jackson views this work as a "mulatto manifesto" that
serves to affirm and awaken Africanicity within a Latin American context:

> These recent writings are about affirmation, not denial, and in this vein
> he wrote *¡Levántate mulato!*, to date the most important statement on the
> Afro-Hispanic identity as well as a personal search for his own ethnic
> identity. One of his purposes in this work is to place Blackness squarely
> within the traditional context of Latin American mestizaje; it is an hon-
> est defense of triethnicity and its contribution to the development of a
> new America.[4]

For Jackson, a major focus of the work is the author's attempt to rescue,
recapture, and reclaim a collective blackness from the margins of self-
expression. In so doing, Zapata Olivella challenges the masses of Latin
Americans with African blood to take pride in their Africanicity, to

4. Jackson, *Black Writers and the Hispanic Canon*, 59.

openly celebrate and embrace it. In *The Culture of Fiction in the Works of Manuel Zapata Olivella,* Yvonne Captain-Hidalgo echoes Jackson's sentiments affirming the importance of blackness as a literary and extra literary trope in the writings of Zapata Olivella.

However, it is the writer himself who probes the depth of his existence in pursuit of a more complete understanding and recognition of his own racial identity:

> Hybrid or new form of man? Am I truly a traitor to my race? A slippery half-Black, half-Indian? A submissive mulatto? Or simply a mixed-blood American who seeks to defend the identity of his oppressed heritage.
>
> (¿Híbrido o nuevo hombre? ¿Soy realmente un traidor a mi raza? ¿Un zambo escurridizo? ¿Un mulato entreguista? O sencillamente un mestizo americano que busca defender la identidad de sus sangres oprimidas.) (*Levántate,* 21)

As a point of departure, Zapata Olivella presents a history of the Antilles and the Americas beginning with the pre-colonial era. The author catalogs the many Indian tribes, such as the Arawaks and Caribes, who were inhabitants of the New World prior to the late fourteenth and fifteenth centuries. He also discusses the customary habits of indigenous tribes related to intertribal war. One of the primary objectives during wars between the Indian tribes was the capture of women, largely due to their societal role as culture bearers. The goal was to expand the tribe through procreation with the captive women, thereby strengthening the tribe for future battles. Zapata Olivella explains that this customary rule of warfare was common practice in indigenous societies well before the arrival of the Europeans. This practice indicates that racial mixing in the New World was already quite extensive prior to the arrival of Europeans and Africans. In other words, "ethnic mixing" was in practice prior to the year 1492. Zapata Olivella then turns his attention to his native Colombia in an effort to explain his tri-ethnic makeup. In the first part of the autobiography "Los ancestros" (The ancestors), he details the Indian ancestry of his tripartite ethnic background. The indigenous tribes of the Arawaks, Chibchas, and Caribes inhabited the islands and coasts of the Antillean coastline. Zapata Olivella then describes a number of their cultural traditions in order to demonstrate that Europeans were not the initiators of culture and "civilization" in the New World. Through a brief presentation of tribal habits, he reaffirms that there existed a cultural norm in indigenous societies, a norm that provides a sense of identity and a collective "civilization." Zapata Olivella paints a vivid picture of these autochthonous societies, habits, and customs, which he describes in the manner of an ethnographer. For example, the hunting practices of the Arawaks and Caribes and their intimate bond with their natural environment demonstrate a highly evolved society. This depiction recalls the social interdependency of the inhabitants of these indigenous tribes and their cultural communion with nature as depicted in *Tierra*.

The description of pre-colonial culture in the Antilles prepares the reader for Zapata Olivella's account of the arrival of the Europeans to the New World in the region that was later designated *Cartegena de Indias*. Following a brief historical account of the onset of colonialism, the author offers a personalized history of his indigenous lineage:

> My Indian blood, like the totality of mixed Americans who have their roots embedded in the first foray of the Conquest, comes to me by means of my maternal grandmother who was raped in an Indian settlement.

> (Mi sangre india, como en la totalidad de los mestizos americanos que tienen hundidas sus raíses en los primeros asaltos de la Conquista, me viene por la abuela materna violada en una ranchería indígena.) (*Levántate*, 29)

Zapata Olivella acknowledges the introduction of Indian blood into his genetic pool as a result of the Conquest. He also locates the ideology of *mestizaje* with the violation of the indigenous woman by the European conquistadors. As a result of miscegenation, the phenotypic markers that reveal the mixing of Spanish and Indian blood within his family line are in evidence. He speaks of "los ojos oblicuos" (oblique eyes) of his Carib uncles and the long, dark braids of his dark-skinned aunts, mother, and sister.

Additionally, Zapata Olivella explores the complexity of mixing by navigating beyond the parameters of racial and ethnic physical signifiers. The first generations of *mestizos* in his family continue their indigenous cultural practices while assimilating Western behaviors. During the first centuries of colonial rule, the inhabitants appear wholly bicultural:

> In those times, his brother Dionisio, a fisherman, would roll his indigenous cloth around his hips in order to sit down on the banks of the swamp

of Lorica. But my uncle Leoncio, who fled the Sinú for Cartegena, had covered his Indian habits with the ways of the city life. His ancestral cloth was substituted for a pair of pants and a shirt, generally white.

(A esas horas su hermano Dionisio, pescador, se enrollaría la paruma alrededor de la cadera para sentarse a la orilla de la ciénaga de Lorica. Pero mi tío Leoncio, huido del Sinú a Cartegena, había revestido sus hábitos indios con los usos de la ciudad. La paruma ancestral fue substituida por el pantalón y la camisa, generalmente blancos.) (*Levántate*, 31–32)

The second segment of his exposition on his ancestry deals with the "darker" component of his racial composition: his African roots. He begins again with the genesis of "Africanized" subjects in the New World. The first examples of Africanicity injected into the New World experience were the "historical" Pinzón brothers, fictionalized mulattos who represent those Africans who served as captains during Columbus's initial expeditions. The Pinzón mulattos provide evidence of European interaction with colonial Africa prior to their arrival in the New World. Magnus Morner in *Race Mixture in the History of Latin America* concurs that the first Negroid slaves sent to the Americas were Spanish-speaking *ladinos* sent directly from Spain. Their mixed-race status bears witness to practices of miscegenation between Europeans and Africans prior to the close of the fifteenth century. Furthermore, their presence identifies miscegenation as a common practice among males and the replication of that practice in the New World can therefore be placed within the framework of European cultural norms. Zapata Olivella notes that the arrival of continental Africans in the New World occurred during the beginning of the sixteenth century with the transatlantic slave trade. He then rehistoricizes the journey of African slaves, primarily from West Africa, through the middle passage and their subsequent enslavement throughout the Americas.

Relative to his native Colombia, the slave trade was initiated in the late 1580s when the first group of Africans disembarked on the shores of Cartegena, instituting a system that continued roughly until the close of the eighteenth century. To that effect, the author states:

Cartegena of India was the first disembarkation port of Africans from America. Annually more than five ships docked here loaded with prisoners from the most diverse African tribes and cultures: Yolofos, Mandingas, Angolas, Lucumíes, Araráes, Biafras, Yorubas, Ibos, etc.

(Cartegena de Indias era el primer puerto de desembarco de africanos de América. Aquí atracaban anualmente más de cinco barcos cargados de prisioneros de las más variadas culturas y tribus africanas: yolofos, mandingas, angolas, lucumíes, araráes, biafras, yorubas, ibos, etc.) (*Levántate*, 36)

Those tribal men, women, and children brought to Cartegena and its surrounding area introduced African cultural forms into a Colombian context. The author introduces readers to his paternal grandmother, Angela Vasquez, a descendant of the original Africans brought to Colombia during the slave trade. For him, she is the embodiment of African culture. Within the text, it is she who recounts the African cosmological ideology of naming, *nommos*.[5] Because Manuel Zapata Olivella is named in honor of his paternal grandfather, Manuel Zapata Granados, it is believed that the spirit of his grandfather resides within his soul. Zapata Olivella sees this retention of Old World traditions as a form of cultural resistance and survival. He stresses pride in being of African descent throughout this section describing his African roots. Zapata Olivella's racial pride is crucial for the embrace of his "mulattoness." The author reveals that some members of his family allow the presence of Spanish and Indian blood to efface their African ancestry. For Zapata Olivella, however, his African past is deliberately and consciously exalted and celebrated. He attributes the pride in his African heritage to those paternal ancestors who struggled to retain aspects of their culture rather than be totally assimilated into Western culture. An account of comments made by his father left an indelible mark on the young Zapata Olivella's self-image. After making a negative remark about conserving traditions of old, his father admonishes him:

Regarding blackness, I am honored to be black; however, I am not going to renounce my African ancestors, brought here as slaves, nor because of them renounce my race only because you have and consider being a Black man as being less than everything else. You are wrong about that and when one has a clean conscience, the color black is not dishonoring. And in terms of the subject to which you refer, it would be more valuable to know from where and how your parents have come so that you don't insult them by behaving like an ingrate.

5. For further discussion of the concept of naming within an African context, consult John Mbiti's *African Religions and Philosophy*.

(En camino a lo negro, honor tengo yo en serlo, pues yo no voy a renegar de mis antepasados africanos, traídos aquí como esclavos, ni por ello a renunciar de mi raza, sólo porque usted tenga y considere al negro como un ser despreciable. Y en eso se equivoca, pues cuando la conciencia es pura, el color de azabache no deshonra. Y en cuanto al tema al cual me ha referido, más le valdría saber de dónde y cómo se han formado sus padres para que no los insulte comportándose como un irracional.) (*Levántate*, 76)

This rebuke was instrumental in moving Manuel Zapata Olivella toward acceptance and appreciation of his blackness. In the final pages of his autobiography, he refers to a time when he was ten years old, and he and his siblings were ignorant of their racial past. He credits "magical intuition" for pushing them toward recognition of their black identity: "In childhood we went forth apparently blind, magical intuition pushing us towards the origins." (En la infancia marchábamos aparentemente ciegos, la intuición mágica empujándonos hacia los orígenes. *Levántate*, 331) Prior to his awareness of Leopold Sedar Senghor, Aimé Césaire, Leon Damas, and Frantz Fanon, he linked race with intellectual emancipation. His immediate family identified themselves as black, not solely due to their pigmentation, but because of the freethinking ideas of their father. With the guidance of a self-defined Afro-Hispanic father, who instilled the spirit of his African past deep within his soul, Manuel Zapata Olivella, a writer/anthropologist, was linked inevitably to his racial past and accepted his black identity. His Spanish heritage, the result of generational rape and a product of the institution of slavery in the Americas, also flows through his veins, creating an indistinguishably African and Spanish blend of ethnicities.

By manipulating the genre of the autobiographical novel, Manuel Zapata Olivella allows the reader to experience firsthand his personal journey toward racial self-consciousness through the use of memories, anecdotes, testimonies, folklore, and history. I believe it is a manipulation of the genre of the autobiographical novel because Zapata Olivella's story is more historical than conventional autobiographical accounts. He includes an account of the history of the New World, the etiology of consanguinity in the New World, and the journey toward acceptance of one's racial and ethnic heritage. Indirectly, the subtitle alludes to the inclusive nature of the text.

In my opinion, the subtitular words of José Vasconcelos, "Por mi raza hablará el espíritu" (My spirit will speak for my race), are representative of the author's subversive tactics. If one were to deconstruct this epigraph in an Africanized manner and place emphasis on the word *spirit,* the inclusive nature of Zapata Olivella's autobiography would become more comprehensible. The fact that the author's spirit "will speak" for his race suggests, as John Mbiti would probably agree, that "spirit" and "race" are indeed interchangeable terminologies. In that light, they can be read as a singular concept that would nullify the autobiographical "I" and interpose a collective "We" as an understood narrative inference. Again, the objective of this study of *Levántate* is not to justify or nullify the issue of autobiography. However, an examination of how the term *autobiography* is applied to the work facilitates a more global contextualization of the novel, one that places this genre within the literary trajectory of the African diaspora in the Americas. Zapata Olivella thus engages his readers on three distinct levels: regional, national, and global. This tripartite perspective permeates the discourse in works preceding and subsequent to *Levántate.*

Las claves, a series of essays published in 1989, offers yet another perspective on the complexities of postcolonial identity. Again, the point of departure is the initial fusing of African blood with other "bloods" during the colonial encounter. The complexities of constructing an identity for a people resulting from historical miscegenation are explored throughout Zapata Olivella's trilogy and continue in his essays.

Structurally, *Las claves* is a collection of thirty essays divided into five parts that span a chronological period from the pre-Colombian era to the twentieth century. In the introduction, the author notes that the European expedition to Africa and the Americas beginning at the close of the fourteenth century introduced the explorers not only to new corners of the earth, but also to new races of people:

> Towards the end of the fifteenth century with their circular routes navigating to Africa and the discovery of the Americas, the Europeans' vision of the contour of the earth was broadened, but also their knowledge of new human races not described in biblical narratives, whom they did not hesitate to classify as anthropoid species, barbarians and salvages.

> (Las postrimerías del siglo XV con sus viajes de circunvalación al Africa y descubrimiento de América, ampliarían la visión de los europeos sobre el contorno de la tierra, pero también su conocimiento de nuevas razas humanas no descritas en los relatos bíblicos, a los cuales no vacilaron en clasificar como especies antropoides, bárbaras y salvajes.) (*Las claves,* 13)

As an interesting point of departure, Zapata Olivella considers the encounter from both the perspective of the viewer and that of the viewed. The European immediately begins to signify, attaching inferior qualifiers onto the new races. The encountered inhabitants are deemed barbarians and savages based on the standards of European norms. This view of the "others" in light of the "self" sets the parameters of racial attitudes that define the relationship between the encountered and those doing the encountering. The Europeans, through divine instruction, sought to civilize these newly "discovered" barbarians, establishing hegemony in terms of social, political, and religious institutions. As Europeans were introduced to Africa, and Africans to the Americas, interracial interaction created conflicts and misunderstandings. For the purpose of this investigation, the first and the fourth sections of essays in this work appear crucial for a full understanding of the author's perspective on racial identity and identification. Although the remaining sections provide insight into the cultural contributions of Africans in the Americas, the first and fourth parts illustrate the etiology of racial mixing and the onset of racial classification. The end result is a triethnic definition of postcolonial identity in the Americas in the aftermath of the emancipation from slavery.

Genocide, slavery, and servitude are the points of departure for recording the history of the New World conquest. Zapata Olivella concentrates his attention on the relationship between the European, the African, and the indigenous American. Like an architect, he begins by laying the foundations on which to build his arguments. A primary cornerstone is the issue of racial identity and classification resulting from the triangular interaction of Europeans, Africans, and indigenous Americans. The five sections of *Las claves* build toward the ultimate creation of a postcolonial identity for Africans. These sections focus on genocide, miscegenation, slavery, and cultural resistance as the "magic keys" to help us understand the complexity of the Americas.

The first section of essays in *Las claves* is dedicated to the abuses suffered by the indigenous population in the New World and the creation of a new "species," the mestizo, a consequence of the sexual violation of indigenous females. Prior to the eventual annihilation of the indigenous population and the emergence of a new "breed" of people, the native people provided assistance to Europeans, assistance that ensured the success of Spanish, Portuguese, French, and other adventurers in navigating and surviving in the new terrain. The Europeans who set out for the New World faced an unfamiliar environment. They were hindered by the natural habitat and were in dire need of food. Zapata Olivella mentions the aid provided by the Arawaks, the Caribes, the Tapuyas, the Arucanos, the Incas, the Patagones, and others, tribes eventually exterminated by those to whom they rendered assistance. The author then points out that the Europeans first targeted the indigenous male population for elimination: "The extermination was directed selectively towards eliminating the male." (El exterminio estuvo dirigido selectivamente para eliminar a los varones. *Las claves,* 28) In consequence, the women were left vulnerable to the sexual assaults of the Europeans. This led to the creation of hybrid offspring produced by the indigenous female and the European male. In chronicling the destruction of the indigenous population in the New World, Olivella sets the stage for the sexual exploitation of both the indigenous and the African woman.

In his condemnation of the crimes committed against indigenous females, Zapata Olivella bemoans the silence of historians:

The profound harm occasioned upon the Indian woman by brutal sexual harassment will never be able to surface. Still, much would have to be incorporated to this chapter forgotten by psychoanalysts in order to re-create the true causes for that which the Europeans, and more concretely, the Peninsular, compelled their violence against the nude, powerless and chained aborigine virgins, young girls and widows of America.

(Nunca podrá exhumarse el profundo daño ocasionado a la mujer india por el hostigamiento brutal de su sexo. Mucho habría que agregar todavía a este capítulo olvidado por los psicoanalistas para reconstruir las verdaderas causas por las cuales los europeos, y más concretamente los peninsulares, compulsaron su violencia contra las desnudas, impotentes y encadenadas vírgenes, impúberes, gestantes y vuidas aborígenes de América.) (*Las claves,* 33)

Nevertheless, these physical attacks produced oral testimonies of the "crimes" silenced by historians. One of the few accounts to detail the barbaric behavior of the conquistadors is Friar Bartolomé de las Casas's *Brevísima relación de la destrucción de las Indias* (Brief account of the destruction of the indians), published in 1552. In a more deliberate account than Las Casas's, Zapata Olivella explores the possible motivations and justifications for such unjustifiable cruelty: "Finally, we would not end by enumerating excuses that only can be called by one name: the sexual bestiality of the European male." (En fin, no terminaríamos de enumerar excusas que solo tienen un nombre: la bestialidad sexual del europeo. *Las claves*, 34) Clearly, the Europeans' image of the indigenous population mirrored the image they projected of themselves: crude, cruel, immoral barbarians.

In the first section of his essay, Manuel Zapata Olivella introduces the final element responsible for the tri-ethnic composition of people in the Americas: slavery, the appearance of the African in the New World. It is interesting to note that the distinction is poignantly made relative to the role that each group played during the colonial era. Latin American historians as well as chroniclers attest to the fact that the African was brought to the Americas exclusively for the purpose of involuntary labor to replace a dying Indian population. However, the African woman shared the fate of her indigenous counterpart—sexual abuse and rape:

> In the case of the African woman, besides the same humiliation suffered by the Indian woman, the corrupt nature of the civilized European of converting sex into an organized market with the blessing of kings, priests and constitutions would have to be admitted.

> (En el caso de la mujer negra, además de los mismos vejámenes sufridos por la india, habría que agregar el hecho corruptor de los civilizados europeos, de convertir el sexo en mercancía organizada con el beneplácito de reyes, papas y constituciones.) (*Las claves*, 35)

Although the abuse was similar, the motives differed. The violation of indigenous women was motivated by the desire for physical satisfaction. African women, on the other hand, were raped for the purpose of producing a constant and viable work force. This utilitarian dimension compounded the plight of the African woman, suggesting her debasement at the hands of the abusers:

> Neither has there been anyone who has stopped to abysmally reflect on the plight of the African woman. Millions of little girls, daughters, wives, widows and sisters separated from their native home lands violently, their mothers, their fathers, their husbands and brother, from the remains of their children and husbands in order to suffer for the rest of her life the indignity of being sold in order to serve the lust of her purchaser; birthing children knowing that much later they too would be repeatedly harassed with the same suffered fury and indifference.

(No ha habido tampoco quien se haya detenido a reflexionar abismada-
mente sobre el desagarramiento de la mujer africana. Millones de niñas,
hijas, esposas, vuidas y hermanas separadas con violencia de sus tierras,
de sus madres, de sus padres, de sus maridos y hermanos, de los cadáv-
eres de sus hijos y sus esposos para sufrir en el resto de su vida la indig-
nidad de ser vendidas para servir a la lujuria del comprador; procrear
hijos e hijas a sabiendas de que serían más tarde acosados repetidas veces
con el mismo furor y desamor padecidos.) (*Las claves*, 34–35)

The attention given to the atrocities experienced by the African woman
underscores the importance of her forced participation in the arena of
racial mixing. The result of this violence was the emergence and the
further "darkening" of a new breed of inhabitants in the Americas. The
central focus of this first essay in *Las claves* is the origin of the blended
American, definitely a major key to understanding the origin of the
racialized subject in Latin America.

Racial oppression and cultural exploitation continue to be major
points of interest in the subsequent section of essays, "Opresión racial y
explotación cultural" (Racial oppression and cultural exploitation).
Here, the author contrasts the treatment of the African under the
European system and under the U.S. system of slavery, and in so doing,
he reveals many major misconceptions about the African in the New
World. Zapata Olivella challenges assertions that Hispanic masters
were more liberal and humane in their treatment of African slaves than
were Anglo-Saxon masters. He also questions the unsubstantiated notion that the African's ethnic composition rendered him physically su-
perior to the indigenous American.

The third section of essays in *Las claves*, "Creatividad del negro bajo
la opresión" (Black creativity under oppression), deals with the creation of a syncretic culture due to acculturation in the Americas. Zapata
Olivella opens by giving credit to Afro-Hispanic researchers for their
role in affirming the creative role of Africans determined to retain and
affirm their own cultural values in America. Cultural syncretism best
describes the mélange of expression that resulted from a tri-ethnic inter-
change. The tenacity of Africans is particularly hailed. Evidenced are
their efforts to resist Western cultural assimilation through many societal institutions, especially religion. Zapata Olivella believes religion is
what allowed Africans to survive under the institution of slavery. By
holding fast to their African religious heritage, the enslaved were able to
gain strength from their pantheistic beliefs. Africans saw slavery as a

punishment from the gods for their violation of the natural law of the ancestors: "African religions are essentially vitalists. The individual is born and survives in life as a result of an unbreakable pact with the Ancestors who promise to conserve and enrich life." (Las religiones africanas son esencialmente vitalistas. El individuo nace y supervive gracias a un pacto irrecusable con sus Ancestros por el cual se comprometen a conservar y enriquecer la vida. *Las claves,* 98) This unyielding allegiance to the Ancestors is at the core of the African religious identity. The African embraces the notion that his life's quality and longevity are linked directly to his demonstrating respect and reverence for the spirits of the ancestors. This explains the "existentialist" quality of the African religious identity:

> African religions are existentialists. The individual with his family, that one in particular who is designated as an invaluable member, should be governed by thousand-year-old experience. The elder members, parents, ancestors, the repositories of this experience are the legate at the first resort by the gods or the god-like heroes.
>
> (Las religiones africanas son existencialistas. El individuo con su familia, a la cual está adscrito como un miembro indisoluble, debe regirse por la experiencia milenaria. Son los miembros más viejos, los padres, los antecesores directos, los depositarios de esta experiencia, legada en primera instancia por los dioses o los héroes semidivinizados.) (*Las claves,* 98)

The continuation of traditions handed down generationally is seen as a perpetuation of the god-self. This amounts to a form of religious existentialism where the concept of god or gods is deliberately constructed through perpetration of the ancestral values and customs. Members of the lineage, as they mature into elders, eventually join the spirit realm through death and are perceived as gods in turn. Finally, the African religious identity is pantheistic:

> African religions are pantheistic; they conceive the individual as a link in a chain and not the center of the universe, linked to all living creatures: man, animal and plant; to the things that serve him: earth, water, air, fire, constellation. And, as already mentioned, the dead.
>
> (Las religiones africanas son panteístas; conciben el individuo como eslabón de una cadena y no simple ombligo del mundo, vinculado a los demás seres vivientes: hombres, animales, y vegetales; a las cosas que le sirven: tierra, agua, aire, fuego, estrella. Y, ya se ha dicho, a los muertos.) (*Las claves,* 98)

In describing some of the different facets of African religiosity, Zapata Olivella underscores the people's attachment to religion, asserting that it enabled their survival under slavery. He asserts further that the pantheistic quality of African religious thought serves as the material and philosophical basis for the "new religions" found in the New World, all postcolonial and associated with the identity of peoples with mixed heritage such as Voodoo, Candomblé, Macumba, Santería, and Rasatafari.

The fourth series of essays in *Las claves*, "El racismo de casta en la sociedad colonial" (The racism of the caste system in colonial society), focuses on the creation of a racial caste system due to miscegenation. The caste system in Latin America created a false sense of identity linked exclusively to pigmentation. Consequently, tri-ethnic citizens embraced Western Aryan ideologies, obliging many to deny certain aspects of their ethnic makeup. Although the ethnic background of the parents was the determining factor for social classification, skin color allowed one to maneuver between classes. Caste and class became synonymous in that the caste classification determined one's class standing, thus motivating many to deny African roots if their "coloring" allowed them to do so. This fact is evident in postcolonial Latin America today as mulattos, children of Spanish and African blood, have created a "space" for themselves and others that is based on the visual evidence of their racial mixing. In other words, if a mulatto is phenotypically more "Spanish-looking" than African, then that component of his or her racial composition is celebrated at the expense of the other. For the purpose of social mobility and status, non-African ethnic identity is deemed a more valuable socioeconomic and political commodity. This postcolonial construct of identity and ethnic rejection is a result of the many negative images associated with Africans that emerged during colonial rule and have infiltrated the contemporary mindset. Thus, that which is "African" is viewed by the larger society as inferior or the least desired. This prejudice has reverberated through the Americas and has endured colonialism, slavery, and even emancipation. Again, violent and racist interaction among Africans, Indians, and Spaniards engulfs Zapata Olivella's narration:

> Violence and racism constituted, as we have seen, the foundation of Colonial America. Its spirit and stigma stain the genesis and development of all American societies. For more than five hundred years of so-called Christian civilization, the crucifixion of the Indian and the exploitation of the Negro is relived in all daily activities. Upon this cross, their arms

are nailed and are being nailed, their pain is carved and their blood is shed.

(La violencia y el racismo constituyeron, como hemos visto, el fundamento de la colonización de América. Su espíritu, su estigma, mancha la génesis y el desarrollo de todas las sociedades americanas. A lo largo de casi quinientos años de pretendida civilización cristiana, en todos los actos, cotidianamente, se revive la crucifixión del indio y la explotación del negro. Sobre esta cruz se clavaron y clavan sus brazos, se talla su dolor y derrama su sangre.) (*Las claves*, 123)

Using biblical analogy, he compares the violence and exploitation perpetrated against the Indian and the Negro to the heinous acts of violence and exploitation of the Son of God. This hint of religious irony is highly effective in showing the hypocritical nature of those whose mission was to bring Christianity to heathen barbarians. Zapata Olivella sees Christianity and the Church as the instigators of the hierarchical paradigm of caste and class in the Americas. This assertion, echoed by other Latin American scholars, explains the tenacity of postcolonial racial and social identity in the New World and the tendency to reject the tri-ethnic paradigm; one that is historically accurate, culturally applicable, and inherently "American."

Beginning with Spanish conquest and colonization, the concept of "pure blood" became the determinant of class and a designator of postcolonial identity in Latin America. Zapata Olivella notes that the colonizers equated power and authority with purity of blood, a criterion that placed the colonizers themselves at the top of the hierarchy. The status of self degenerates based on the perceived amount of "impure blood." For example, directly below the European colonizers on the social pyramid were their offspring born in the New World. Instead of being classified as "European," they were classified as "criollo" (Creole). This distinction implies that the mere association with non-Spaniards in the New World in some way or another "tainted" the blood of all those conceived on its soil, rendering them inferior. As Zapata Olivella points out, the result was a system of European supremacy based on "bloodlines."

As colonial America became more and more "impure," a caste system of racial classification based on ancestral line became more intricate and codified. Mexican scholar Gonzalo Aguirre Beltrán identifies the division of classes based on racial/ethnic composition, with the power concentrated among those at the top. Borrowing from Beltrán, Zapata Olivella in *Las claves* lists the hierarchy of miscegenation thus:

1. Español con india, mestizo.
2. Mestiza con español, castizo.
3. Castizo con española, español.
4. Español con negra, mulato.
5. Mulata con español, morisco.
6. Morisco con española, chino.
7. Chino con india, salta atrás.
8. Salta atrás con mulata, lobo.
9. Lobo con china, gíbaro.
10. Gíbaro con mulata, albarazado.
11. Albarazado con negra, cambujo.
12. Cambujo con india, zambaigo.
13. Zambaigo con loba, calpa mulato.
14. Calpa mulato con cambuja, tente en el aire.
15. Tente en el aire con mulata, no te entiendo.
16. No te entiendo con india, torna atrás. (*Las claves*, 128)

The adopted Mexican model of caste taxonomy for those in all of the Americas is a result of the intermingling of the European, Indian, and African Zapata Olivella's summation of such classification is a testament to the level of "mixing" that took place in the Americas. Magnus Morner in *Race Mixture in the History of Latin America* presents an almost identical configuration of racial categories in New Spain during the eighteenth century. The structure of the hierarchy is interesting in that the mixed-race progeny of the Spanish and the Indian are placed at the very top of the paradigm. In other colonies of the Americas, Portuguese, Dutch, or British occupy the top. Consequently, "Indian" refers to the indigenous populace in this stratification. At the bottom are those considered unclassifiable (No te entiendo), that is to say that the offspring of an "unclassifiable" and an Indian woman is beyond the range of social recognition. As stated above, this matrix is an example of the degree of racial mixing that took place in the Americas, and it parallels social positionality. Embedded within these systems is the Olivellian concept of tri-ethnicity. To this end, Zapata Olivella states that one's ethnic characteristic was as important as, if not more so than, the surname.

The fifth and final section of essays in *Las claves* is devoted to the author's perspectives on the social status of Europeans, creoles, mulattos, mestizos, zambos, pure blacks, and Indians as a result of miscegenation. Zapata Olivella focuses on the period from emancipation to Latin American independence and beyond in describing the social interaction between the multiethnic members of this society. The author returns to the issue of second-class citizenship and the non-Europeans who were relegated to it and chronicles the plight of the enslaved prior to liberation.

After having provided a historical account of the struggle for societal acceptance by blacks, Indians, and people of mixed blood as they moved from abolition, manumission, and independence in Latin America, Zapata Olivella considers the present state of racial matters in the Americas. He concludes that the existing reality links racism to racial composition. As a result, mixed-race people of the Americas have had to negotiate their status depending on their own sense of racial identity. In a more personal examination, Zapata Olivella discusses the modern-day racism that exists in his home country, Colombia:

> In Colombia, as in other Latin countries where there is a recognizable black population, the general attitude is one of negating the existence of racial problems. "There is no racial discrimination here," is the confession that is advanced in an intent to evade the subject. From then on, this cover-up by whites and mestizos, accepted unconsciously and clearly, including by a majority of those of African descent, isn't anything other than the interjection of the old scale of values of white supremacy. In schools, clubs, public establishments, in politics, colleges and universities, as well as in the factories and other activities, we find black people in one form or another incorporated into the socio-cultural process. But, this is not to negate the existence of discriminatory practices in a republican order that has perpetuated the privileges and prejudices of colonial society.

> (En Colombia, como en otros países latinos donde hay una reconocida población negra, la actitud general es la de negar la existencia de problemas raciales. "Aquí no hay discriminación racial", es la confesión que se adelanta a cualquier intento de abortar el tema. Desde luego, este encubrimiento por parte de blancos y mestizos, aceptado inconsciente o lúcidamente, inclusivo por la mayoría de descendientes africanos, no es otra cosa que la introyección de la vieja escala de valores de la supremacía blanca. En la escuela, clubes, establecimientos públicos, en la política, colegios y universidades, así como en las fábricas y otras actividades, encontramos negros, en una forma u otra incorporados al proceso socio-cultural. Pero eso no niega la existencia de prácticas discriminatorias en

un orden republicano que ha perpetuado los privilegios y prejuicios de la sociedad colonial.) (*Las claves,* 174)

Zapata Olivella uses the familiar as a means to illustrate the general. The refrain, "there is no racism here," is one that Zapata Olivella hears reverberating throughout Latin America. The denial of the existence of racism is equated to an act of Western hegemony reminiscent of colonial rule. Whites and mestizos are motivated to deny racial prejudice in Latin America in order to discredit what a majority of blacks and mulattos have protested against. Zapata Olivella sees denial as a form of neocolonialism that allows for the continuation of white supremacy. He argues further that visible signs indicating the social integration of blacks are not an adequate indicator of the elimination of racial prejudice or a diminishment of privileges afforded to whites as the legacy of colonial rule.

Zapata Olivella argues that the colonial mentality in postcolonial Latin America persists. Postcolonial concepts of racial identity and identification continue to plague Latin America as its inhabitants struggle to understand themselves and the complex society in which they were born and raised. In this series of essays, Zapata Olivella declares that the social situation for nonwhites is not that far removed from their societal predicament during colonial rule. *Changó, Levántate,* and *Las claves* illustrate his belief that miscegenation among the European, Indian, and African created a cultural plurality in Latin America that racialized social position. This social paradigm was the impetus for the creation of a white supremacist caste system designed to maintain racial, social, economic, and political control in the Americas. This trilogy of works represents Zapata Olivella's attempts to detail the historical development of postcolonial racial identity and classification. These three works, in particular, advance the author's theories regarding the creation of postcolonial identity in the Americas that is tri-ethnic in constitution resulting from historical miscegenation.

Chapter VI

From the Americas to Africa

Hemingway, the Death Stalker

The last decade of the twentieth century was a fruitful one for Manuel Zapata Olivella. He produced novels, plays, short fiction, and critical essays. In the twenty-first century, Zapata Olivella continued to work until his death in November 2004. His contributions to Latin American literature and culture span over fifty years, having begun in 1949 with his first published work, *Tierra*.

In 1997, Zapata Olivella published another collection of essays, *Rebelión*, a compilation of some of the most critical expository writing produced by this writer. The essays reflect the author's centering of blackness and his focus on the racial/ethnic composition of the Latin American subject. It is safe to say that his literary contributions are substantial and his black-centered literary aesthetic is in full bloom. This work, as well as the author's latest published work to date, *El árbol brujo de la libertad: Africa en Colombia—orígenes, transculturación, presencia, ensayo histórico-mítico* (2002), revisits one of the major points of contestation in the Americas: the construction of race and racial identity. In a collection of five sections, Zapata Olivella continues to expose ideologies resulting in the vilification and annihilation of the Amerindian and its erasure from colonial history. Zapata Olivella dedicates parts of this work to a rearticulation of his belief that the conquest of the Americas by Europeans was the beginning of the demise of Amerindian culture and civilization. As in *Las claves,* the destruction and demolition of an empire is linked to the exploitation and manipulation of indigenous peoples as Europeans terrorized the New World in their efforts to control and subordinate this newly encountered domain. *Rebelión* also addresses the role of the African in the development of the Americas. The institution of slavery and its aftermath are a central focus in many of the essays in this volume as Zapata Olivella discusses the major cultural contributions of people of African decent in the New World. Essays such as "La más vieja raíz de

110

la humanidad" (The oldest human race), "La africanidad, memoria ancestral" (Africanicity, ancestral memory), and "Negra de las Americas"
(Black woman of the Americas) bring to the forefront the importance of
the history of Africans in the Americas. The major theme of the collection, one that permeates each chapter and represents an amalgamation
of the whole, is the biological mixing of those in the Americas and the
birth of a mixed-race people who represent the future population of these
defined geographical spaces. For Zapata Olivella, an "American" is one
who is multiethnic. This author of mixed ethnic ancestry calls for the
cultural celebration of the multiethnic whole, encouraging each ethnic
identity to maintain the cultural manifestations embedded in the religion, music, food, and traditions of its culture. Zapata Olivella believes
that the understanding of the history of racial and ethnic mixing is the
magic key to understanding and celebrating human diversity. The concluding lines of the volume reveal the author's hypothesis on the future
of global race and ethnic discourse:

> Upon speaking about the future presence of an Amerindian-Afro-
> European ethnicity, so much in America than outside of her, only
> demonstrates to us the conviction that the multiracial American phe-
> nomenon will continue to generate new genetic types and codes. It is not
> sufficient for us to envision at the dawn of the 21st century a predomi-
> nant race, whatever its characteristics or origin. However, this does not
> imply that the ethnic consciousness of people will disappear; however,
> recent historical events show us how it continues to grow more and
> more; through that consciousness one will arrive at a more diverse and
> clearer commitment to universal brotherhood.

> (Al hablar de una presencia futura de la etnia amerindo-afroeuropea,
> tanto en América, como fuera de ella, sólo nos mueve el convencimiento
> de que el fenómeno multirracial americano continuará generando
> nuevos tipos y códigos genéticos. No alcanzamos a vislumbrar en el
> horizante del siglo XXI una raza predominante, cualesquiera que sean
> sus características u orígenes. Sin embargo, esto no implica que vaya a
> desaparecer la conciencia étnica de los pueblos; antes bien, los aconte-
> cimientos históricos recientes nos muestra cómo ella va creciendo cada
> vez más; a través de esa conciencia se llegará a un más profundo con-
> ocimiento de la diversidad humana y a una más lúcida compromiso con
> la fraternidad universal.) (*Rebelión*, 367–68)

In 1991, Zapata Olivella published *Hemingway*, a fictional work about
the life of the prize-winning American writer. In this text, the Afro-

Colombian author goes beyond the Africa-centered focus that characterizes his later works of fiction. His perspective shifts this work to the continent of Africa, exposing her rich traditions, superstitions, and myths. *Hemingway* veers thematically and aesthetically away from social realism and protest in the Americas in order to concentrate on aesthetic innovations. Blackness remains a central preoccupation to the text (the action is centered in Africa, principally Kenya; African mythology and tribal traditions are an integral part of the narration), but the work is clearly more aesthetic than problematic.

The text is centered on the escapades of humans as they invade the world of animals for scientific and journalistic purposes. Africa and her environs become the setting for this European invasion by thrill-seekers and explorers. Of particular interest is the dependence of Hemingway and his entourage on the native Kenyans to explain and interpret nature and the animal kingdom. To Zapata Olivella, the manner in which the Kikuyo, the Masai, and other African tribes navigate the terrain exemplifies the African way of interacting with their environment. The text depicts a people familiar with nature and its inhabitants and respectful of both. When this respect is violated, nature retaliates. I would rank *Hemingway* among the best written and emotionally stimulating of this author's works. The sense of African adventure is intriguing, and makes the reader an active participant in the escapades of the fictional Hemingway and his comrades.

Hemingway is written in the form of a travel narration and is broken down into six parts. It is a fictional chronicle of the challenges and adventures of Hemingway in his quest for the *Mamut Sagrado* (sacred mammal). Included in the novel's front matter is a proviso intended to distance the fiction from reality: "The characters, situations and narrative voices of this novel are made up. Whatever similarity or coincidence with historical persons belongs to the world of literary fiction." (Los personajes, situaciones y voces narratives de esta novela son fabulados. Cualquier parecido o coincidencia con personajes históricos pertenecen al mundo de la ficción. *Hemingway*) However, as the fictional life of Ernest Hemingway unfolds within the text, documentable biographical truths about Hemingway are included as well, giving the text a certain level of "believability." It is the element of verisimilitude that encourages the reader to confuse fiction and history and to approach the text as if it were a nonfictional account.

The narration is cyclical: the work begins in 1961, in the Mayo

Clinic in Rochester, and moves backward, only to culminate in the same time frame as when the novel began. Through the use of flashbacks, interior monologues, and scatological and sexual dialogue, the reader journeys through time, place, and space as the exploits of Hemingway, who is accompanied by colleagues and tribal Africans, are narrated. Africa and her total cosmology are interwoven into the lives of all the major characters as Hemingway engages with the "natural" environment.

As the characters journey toward Mount Kenya, many underlying stories or subplots surface that contribute to the dominant event, the quest for the Sacred Mammal. On safari, Hemingway and his cohorts search for the animal. During their pursuit, the characters discuss African cultural tradition, superstition, love, sex, death, massacres, tribal wars, and suicide. The major characters, Ernest Hemingway, Renata, and Antoñete, are involved in a ménage à trois or triangular relationship. Supporting characters include the mysterious Kamau Johnstone, the British Commissioner Alex Smith, nature, elephants, and other creatures in the wild.

The story begins with Hemingway in the Mayo Clinic, semiconscious. The date is April 15, 1961. The reader is informed that Hemingway recently returned from a safari in Kenya. During the safari, his role was that of a scientific reporter and not a hunter. The first-person narrator, presumably the voice of Hemingway, states that the mission was to record data about elephants and other mammals at the highest altitudes of Mount Kenya. As the senses of the reader are titillated with descriptions of the dichotomous smell of chloroform and the perfume of flowers that permeate the hospital room, the idea that Hemingway may be deranged or psychotic emerges. Moreover, we are not sure as to the circumstances of his confinement. Is he in intensive care? Is he on a psychiatric ward? The reader is eager to learn the physical and mental condition of this famous protagonist whose thoughts of Renata, Antoñete, elephants, lions, and bullfighters run wild. The reader also learns about the Sacred Mammal, the beast that has consumed the thoughts of the physically and mentally wounded protagonist. A semidelirious Hemingway tries to explain to the attending physician that he feels the weight of a lead bullet lodged in the base of his brain (*Hemingway*, 11). Later in the text, Hemingway connects the sensation of having been wounded with the notion that he has wounded the sacred animal: "But I feel the weight of the bullet and it is not a false perception . . . it happens that yesterday I wounded the Sacred Mammal precisely in the back fold of its ear, and of course, the path of the bullet was another." (Pero siento el peso de la bala y no es ninguna percepción falsa . . . resulta que ayer herí al Mamut Sagrado precisamente en el surco posterior de su oreja, y claro, el recorrido del proyectil fue otro, *Hemingway,* 11) The psychological manifestation of the pain of the protagonist, the reader learns later in the text, is the manifestation of a Kikuyo myth about the sacred mammal. Kikuyo legend states that shooting at el Mamut Sagrado shortens one's life (es acortar el camino, *Hemingway,* 301). Thus, as the work begins, the reader assumes the role of a detective trying to piece together the clues provided in this first chapter. In the second chapter, we move back in time and back to Africa.

It is 8:00 A.M. early October. The protagonist is waiting in King George's Airport in Nairobi, Kenya, for the arrival of his two expedition partners, one from Spain (Antoñete) and the other from Italy (Renata). Frustrated, he learns that both flights will arrive hours late. In the disruption of the narration, a new character, Alex Smith, is presented. It is revealed that Alex is a longstanding friend of Hemingway's who accompanied him on previous safaris in Africa. Prior to serving as police commissioner, Smith was chief of the Tsavo National Park rangers. He has come to the airport to assist Hemingway and his comrades, and it is through this narration that the reader learns that Hemingway has come to Kenya in the capacity of a "scientific reporter" along with colleagues, Renata and Antoñete. Hemingway is presented as a middle-aged adventurer who returns to Africa not to kill on safari, but to gather information on a specific mission. Hemingway, a thrill-seeker, longs for the ultimate life experience: the capture of the legendary beast referred to in African mythology, a beast many have not seen.

The first reference to Renata occurs when Hemingway is in the hospital, semi-conscious, contemplating past events. Her name emerges from his confused thoughts of her, and a term of endearment, "El Viejo Toro" (the old bull), comes to mind. Renata is described as a vibrant and jubilant twenty-year-old who is the daughter of friends of Hemingway's. Her role on the mission is to photograph feats of elephants as well as the Sacred Mammal at certain elevations of Mount Kenya. With Renata, Zapata Olivella revisits a dominant leitmotif in his work: racial mixing. She is the product of two continents, cultures, and worlds: Europe and Africa. Her father was an Italian soldier and her mother an Eritrean. As a result of this union, Renata sees herself as the daughter of war and the forest: "I am the daughter of war and forest . . .

portraying the sexual act of animals is as if I were reviving memories of
my own fertilization in a thicket." (Soy hija de la guerra y de la selva . . .
retratar la cópula de los animales es como si reviviera mi propia fecun-
dación en un matorral. *Hemingway*, 29) The sexual attraction between
Hemingway and Renata surfaces early in the narrative, paralleling sex
and sexual attraction in the animal kingdom. Physical attraction between Hemingway and Renata occurs during their first embrace:

> Vibrant and jubilant, well seasoned for her 20 years, Renata had me
> prisoner between her arms. She did not stop looking at me in the face
> and there is where she directed her eyes—on my ashen eyebrows, on my
> beard, my lips—she deposited her arousing kisses. I, who have always
> been impetuous with the daughters of Eve, experienced certain insecu-
> rity faced with her harassment. In order to appear sincere, I did not be-
> lieve myself worthy of that young creature who was giving herself over
> to a man so surpassing in age.

> (Vibrante y jubilosa, bien sazonados sus veinte años, Renata me tenía
> prisionero entre sus brazos. No dejaba de mirarme la cara y allí donde
> dirigía sus ojos—en mis cejas cenicientas, en la barba, sobre los labios—
> depositaba sus acalorados besos. Yo que siempre he sido impetusos con
> las hijas de Eva, experimenté cierta inseguridad frente a su acoso. Para
> ser sincero, no creía merecer aquella criatura juvenil que se entregaba
> tan ciega a un hombre bastante aventajado en edad.) *(Hemingway*, 18–19)

Ernest Hemingway, the writer, had a reputation as a ladies man. His
fascination with women is a result of his early twentieth-century ideology of manhood. This ideology included dependency on and exploitation of the opposite sex. Linda Wagner-Martin states that as critics
continue to delve into the persona of Hemingway, it becomes clear "that
Hemingway was a product of his time—and those times were marked
with a nearly obsessive interest in sexuality and erotica."[1] However, in
Zapata Olivella's text, Renata is portrayed as the pursuer. She is described as holding Hemingway captive, a prisoner in her arms. Her
fixed stare at the parts of his face suggests desired intimacy with his
countenance. The kisses she deposits on his face are filled with passion
and sexual desire. The text implies that Hemingway, quite familiar with
such advances, tries to deny the embedded messages encoded in the

---

1. Linda Wagner-Martin, "The Romance of Desire in Hemingway's Fiction,"
in *Hemingway and Women: Female Critics and the Female Voice*, ed. Laurence R. Broer
(Birmingham: University of Alabama Press, 2004), 54.

embrace and kisses; however, male physiology overrules cognitive will as his body responds to the advances despite the age barrier separating the two. Sexual symbolism and metaphors run amok in their initial encounters. The first embrace itself is laced with sexual imagery: "Each time that I placed my hairy arm on her sensitive skin it quivered shivered, my mouth opened instinctively for the kiss. My 'Erotic Gazelle!' I responded when she provocatively calls me 'Old Bull' for the first time, inciting my last leaps of satire." (Cada vez que ponía mi brazo velludo sobre su piel sensible vibraba estremecida, la boca abierta por el instinto del beso. ¡Mi "Gacela Erótica"!, le respondí cuando provocativa me llamo por vez primera "Viejo Toro", incitando mis últimos brincos de sátiro. *Hemingway*, 27) The reference to "Erotic Gazelle" evokes an erotic sexualization of Renata. Her bestial allure is compared to that of one of the most graceful and beautiful animals in the wild. And, as the king of the animal kingdom is constantly in pursuit of this delicacy, so is Hemingway, the hunter, in pursuit of human prey. Conversely, her nickname for him, "Bull," connotes sexual prowess, dominance, strength, and virility, all conventional signs of manliness. Zapata Olivella's mastery of erotic narration is skillfully displayed throughout the novel. In chapter seven, for example, during a photo shoot, Renata is capturing a traditional ritual of adolescents of the Kikuyo tribe, "juego de amor" (love game). During this ceremony, the young girls of the tribe perform a sacred dance in the nude in the shallow of the river. As Renata photographs the dance, Hemingway looks on as the tribal adolescent boys behold the captivating performance. Her film having run out, Renata and Hemingway perform a love dance of their own:

> The roll of film exhausted, Renata turns towards me, stretched out, bare feet, pretended to sleep. Silently she placed her hand through my waistband and with the warm spider of her fingers she electrified the most hidden pores. Then, assured that I was not asleep, she excited me with her lips, parched for bitterness and syrup. I reacted with the innocence of the primordial Adam, evoking my first sexual experience.

> (Agotado el rollo de película, Renata volvió hasta mí, que tendido, los pies descalzos, simulaba dormir. Sigilosamente introdujo su mano por mi pretina y con la calurosa araña de sus dedos electrizó los más escondidos poros. Entonces, segura de que no dormía, me hurgó con sus labios, sedienta de hiel y almíbar. Reaccioné con la inocencia del primigenio Adán, evocando mi primera experiencia sexual.) (*Hemingway*, 64)

The figurative language and symbolic metaphors illustrate Zapata Olivella's talent for evocative imagery. The hands and fingers of Renata are metamorphosed and compared to the legs of a spider, whose many parts invade Hemingway's manhood, causing goose bump-like pleasure with every caress. This quite scintillating scene ends with the two engaging in sexual intercourse beneath the water in full daylight and "wading in its afterglow" (El punto de apoyo para que nuestros cuerpos copularan, como la "Gacela Erótica lo quería, bajo las aguas a plena luz." *Hemingway*, 65). Renata's advances cause Hemingway to reflect on his experience with the Cherokee prostitute who stole his virginity. Renata is thus linked to his sexual awakening, and she is cast throughout the novel as a wholly sexual being.

Antoñete Palma is the third major character introduced in the novel. He is Hemingway's godson. Antoñete's parents, Belén and Cayetano, were friends of Hemingway's during his stay in Spain. Antoñete is a biologist who has joined the mission, and his character personifies the voice of science. Antoñete can be found manipulating scientific jargon, expounding at length on the technical name and historical genealogy of animals encountered during the safari. He becomes part of a ménage à trois as the three principal characters engage in an emotional tug-of-war. Antoñete's character is the antithesis of Hemingway's. Antoñete's father wanted him to become a writer like his godfather: "Pídale a la Virgen que me lo haga escritor como su padrino" (*Hemingway*, 26), and not a bullfighter like his father. However, Antoñete's hereditary inclination to the sport is revealed when a buffalo, separated from the herd, confronts Hemingway, Renata, Antoñete, and the rest of the party. Antoñete comments that the buffalo is ripe for bullfighting. In order to demonstrate his masculinity, Antoñete takes a red cape and challenges the startled animal, but his demonstration of male virility fails before a disinterested adversary: "The mocked beast left staring against an empty space that was never advised. Standing, shouting at it, Antoñete hoped that it returned to the deceit. But the buffalo without caste didn't even look back. Upon seeing that it was fleeing, he rolled up the cape, his eyes daring like a boy." (La bestia burlada se fue a estrellar contra un vacío que no avisorara nunca. De pie, gritándole, Antoñete esperaba que retornara al engaño. Pero el búfalo sin casta ni siquiera miró atrás. Al ver que huía, arrojó la carpa, ardidos los ojos como un niño. *Hemingway*, 142)

Hemingway upstages Antoñete's sexuality and manhood in the novel.

Antoñete is seen as a serious scientific scholar. Nevertheless, his attraction to Renata creates a sexual conflict among the three principal characters. Again, their sexual attraction is linked to animals. In an attempt to assert female social and sexual superiority over males, Renata engages in banter with Antoñete that ignites their animalistic lust. A description of how the female mantis devours her partner after sex and a discussion of the sexual life of a queen bee lead to masturbation and a sexually stimulated biologist: "Passion and thirst became partners in open complicity in order to inflame erotic hunting. The young biologist tried to hide his hunger with scientific subterfuge." (El calor y la bebida se asociaron en franca complicidad para enardecer la carcería erótica. El joven biólogo pretendía esconder su hambre con el subterfugio científico. *Hemingway,* 114) However, the young biologist is emasculated, yet again, when Hemingway chastises him: "Look for another whore! Take yourself to the nearest brothel and win her over like I did! You have to take her with your bare hands as I took mine!" (—¡Busca a otra puta! ¡Marchate al burdel cercano y enamórala como yo! ¡Has de ganártela a puro pulso como he conquistado la mía! *Hemingway,* 268) In the end, Antoñete cannot compete with Hemingway in the sexual arena or with his father in the bullfighting ring. Sadly, his desire to prove himself in both arenas ultimately leads to his ironic death.

A final character worthy of analysis is the Sacred Mammal itself, *el Mamut Sagrado.* This mammal serves as a unifying element in the novel and is responsible for the demise of the three main characters. It is also representative of African cultural traditions. The first reference to the Sacred Mammal occurs when Hemingway is in the Mayo Clinic, and references continue throughout the work. The beast takes center stage in the fourth part of the work, "El Mamut Sagrado," and constitutes the turning point in the narrative.

The section begins as Hemingway and his companions arrive at the foot of Mount Kenya. As they begin their ascent, they are amazed by the awesome natural beauty of the snowcapped mountains and the creatures that inhabit them. Stillness and silence surround their climb as if they were treading on sacred or majestic ground. Tribal people believe the mountains possess deitylike qualities. Additionally, those who inhabit the mountain, such as the Wa-Ndoboro people, feel intimately connected to nature. However, Hemingway and his band consider the tribal people barbarous savages and fear that they are on the verge of being attacked. It is the Europeans, however, who are the invaders:

A few women carried their young on their hips. This calmed me, looking as if they were not ready for war. That did not stop my worry. The scars and tattoos on their faces and stomachs revealed their savagery. The males watched us with the fixed stare of hunters. Tall, round muscles. With small steps, the Suk fell to the ground and addressed the one that appeared to be the chief. Accompanied with gestures, he emitted clicking sounds similar to the chirping of birds. After a long silence in which the elders exchanged stares, the chief responded with sharp sibilants. Mukula was limited to transmitting to me the response. —We have violated their territory.

(Algunas madres cargaban a sus pequeños sobre las caderas. Este hecho me tranquilizó, al parecer no estaban en pie de la guerra. No por ello dejaron de preocuparme. Las cicatrices y tatuajes en caras y vientres revelaban su salvajismo. Los varones nos observaban con la mirada fija de los cazadores. Altos, los músculos rollizos. Con pasos medidos, el suk cayó al suelo y se dirigió al que parecía ser el jefe. Acompañándose de gestos, emitió chasquidos semejantes al piar de los pájaros. Después de un largo silencio en que los más viejos intercambiaron sus miradas, el jefe le respondió con agudos sibilantes. Mukula se limitó a transmitirme su respuesta. —Hemos violado su territorio.) (*Hemingway*, 216–17)

This citation is critical for many reasons. First, it displays the ideology of Western hegemony in the midst of an example of African civilization and cultural normality. Second, this quote is an example of the author's use of human ecology. The gestures and communicative mode of the Wa-Ndoboro chief exemplify the level to which this group of people have become one with its surroundings. The speech pattern of the natives is presented as being similar to the songs of birds. Finally, this textual reference affirms the Europeans' violation of space and place. The leader of the Wa-Ndoboro tribe warns that the "outsiders" have violated their territory. This "violation" is not only geographical, it is also against nature. The Wa-Ndoboro informs Hemingway and his group that their quest violates the sanctity of nature and demonstrates irreverence to nature.

The group of "hunters" proceeds, encountering elephants, leopards, and other forms of life on Mount Kenya. Finally, Hemingway has his first encounter with the Sacred Mammal. However, the manner of this encounter leaves the reader questioning the reality of it. After having had his usual shots of whisky, the protagonist begins his account by confusing reality and fiction:

If that night in the Valley of Eternal Clarity even though left with doubts of lucidity when I was sinking slowly into the state of unconsciousness by an overdose of whisky, now, returned to the world of reality, or of death, I consider alive and certain what then I saw, felt and did, belonging or not to the realm of myth.

(Si el aquella noche en la Valle de Eterna Claridad aún me quedaban rescoldos de lucidez cuando me hundía lentamente en las tinieblas del inconsciente por una sobredosis de whisky, ahora, vuelto al mundo de la realidad o de la muerte, doy por vivido y cierto lo que entonces vi, sentí y ejecuté, pertenezca o no al reino de la fábula.) (*Hemingway*, 269)

Episodic encounters exemplify the level of blurring in the text evidenced in subsequent fictional accounts. Hemingway's credibility is called into question as a result of his mental and physical condition. Hemingway claims to have heard the sound of a mammoth creature approaching him, but he saw no trace of its advancing. The protagonist states that he grabbed his rifle in fear and awaited the appearance of the beast. Suddenly, out of the haze the bulk of the Sacred Mammal appeared, his hide ruddy and moldy from the moss of centuries. Hemingway fired and wounded the animal, and this reminded Hemingway of the curse of the Kikuyo legend: "Imperturbable, it advanced without altering the slow and deliberate rhythm of death that is not rushed or stopped. I then remembered the Kikuyo legend and repentant, I understood that I had shot at myself." (Imperturbable avanzó sin alterar el ritmo lento y pausado de la muerte que no se precipita ni detiene. Recordé entonces la leyenda kikuyo y arrepentido, comprendí que había disparado contra mí mismo. *Hemingway*, 271) It is at this moment in the novel that Hemingway acknowledges and accepts the mythology of the African legend. He embraces the superstitions of the African people, and the prophesy begins to be fulfilled. Whether a manifestation of delirium, hallucination, or conscious reality, the existence of the Sacred Mammal is confirmed in Hemingway's mind. He was sure that the shots from his rifle inflicted harm on the beast, and he understood the consequences of his action.

The latter chapters of the fourth part of the novel recount the death of Antoñete. Ironically, his death confirms his father's fear that his son would take up the sport of bullfighting. When the group encounters a herd of rhinoceros, Antoñete imagines that one of them is a bull, and Mount Kenya is transformed into a bullring in Andalusia. As Antoñete

begins to encourage the animal, the startled rhino defends itself.
Antoñete opens the cape about his feet, ready to swing the cape away
from the rhino as if it were a bull, like he had seen his father do as a boy.
As Antoñete and the rhino square off, Hemingway grabs his rifle and
prepares to protect the son of the famed bullfighter. The rhino retreats,
but there soon appears a second rhino that no one has seen; he gores
the bullfighting biologist. Renata rushes to his aid while Hemingway
fires at the raging animal. Antoñete's last words to Renata evoke the
curse of the Wa-Ndoboro. He warns her that the revenge of the *Mamut
Sagrado* is upon them. The narration comes full circle as Renata's flight
is delayed the same amount of time it had been delayed at the beginning of the work. The reader is then returned to the Mayo Clinic.

As Hemingway concludes the "funeral" ceremony for the cremated
body of Antoñete, he informs Renata that the flight to Rome departs in
ten minutes. Aware that Renata is pregnant, Hemingway wistfully contemplates the first flight of his unborn child as the two depart for Rome.
However, neither mother nor child arrives home. An officer informs
Hemingway that the flight crashed in the sea, leaving no survivors. The
news of the death of Renata and his unborn child devastates Hemingway
and he looks to his friend Alex for support. However, Alex is suffering
his own trauma. He had been having an affair with his sister-in-law,
who was aboard the same flight. As both men grieve, they turn to whisky
for temporary relief. Hemingway then leaves for Spain, reflecting on the
vengeance of the Sacred Mammal. For the first time, he begins to feel the
weight of the bullet lodged in his head: "At an altitude of fifteen thousand
feet, carrying Antoñete's remains, and above the Mediterranean, Renata
and my son's grave, I felt the weight of the bullet lodged in my head for the
first time." (A quince mil pies de altura, llevando el cadáver de Antoñete, y
sobre el Mediterráneo, sepultura de Renata y de mi hijo, sentí por primera
vez el peso de la bala crustada en mi cerebro. *Hemingway*, 305)

While waiting to leave Nairobi with the ashes of Antoñete,
Hemingway contemplates suicide. While in the airport, he learns that
he must acquire a license in order to take his guns out of the country:

Guns? It was the necessary and just symbol of how I was to hurt myself.
In the brief recapitulation that I made of my whole life in that instance,
the necessary time that suicide takes to lift the gun and shoot oneself, I
summarized my childhood, youth, wars, novels, country, safari, all em-
bodied in those arms.

(¿Fusiles? Era símbolo preciso y justo de cuanto me hería. En la breve re-capitulación que hice de toda mi vida en aquel instante, el tiempo nece-sario que se toma el suicida para levantar el arma y disparase, resumí mi infancia, juventud, guerras, novelas, patria, safari, todo encarnado en esas armas.) (*Hemingway*, 299)

In Spain, Hemingway reunites with his friends Cayetano and Belén Palma, parents of Antoñete. During their sad reunion, Hemingway learns why his friend asked that he pray that Antoñete become a writer like his godfather and not a bullfighter. Ironically, a gypsy predicted that Cayetano would be gored to death by a bull: a fate that awaited his first-born son.

Hemingway instinctively knows that his life is over. He becomes delirious and is haunted by visions of the Sacred Mammal. Hemingway engages in conversation with the beast and hallucinates:

I have on my side the double-barreled Richardson shotgun. It has been many years since it has accompanied me in my solitude. At one moment or another it will come for me. I know that it courts and follows my steps. When was the last time that I saw it? That I don't even remember! It pursues me hidden within me! Kenya! Spain! The United States! I am a bull that tries to flee when my paths are closed. Suddenly, the blind alley-way that leads to the bloody plaza of memories opened up to me, where death dressed in its suit of lights waits for me.

(Tengo a mi lado la carabina *Richardson* de dos cañones. Hace muchos años que me acompaña en mi soledad. De un momento a otro vendrá por mí. Sé que ronda y sigue mis pasos. ¿Cuándo lo vi por última vez? ¡Ni siquiera eso recuerdo! ¡Me persigue oculto en mi mismo! ¡Kenia! ¡España! ¡Estados Unidos¡ Soy un toro que trata de huir cuando los caminos están clausurados. De repente, se me abre el callejón que con-duce a la plaza ensangrentada de los recuerdos, donde me espera la muerte con su vestido de luces.) (*Hemingway*, 333–34)

In the last episode of the work, the narration returns to 1961, four months after the initial encounter with the protagonist in chapter one. The location has shifted from Rochester, Minnesota, to Ketchum, Idaho. The narration becomes increasingly hallucinogenic or oneiric. In a dreamlike state of consciousness, perhaps under the influence of anti-depressants, Hemingway envisions a herd of elephants invading his room. The elephants watch him in silence. As he tries and fails to flee, Hemingway notices that the animals appear more like dwarf mammals than elephants. When they begin flapping their ears, he calls out to Alex Smith for help. The apparition informs him that he is in Ketchum, thousands of miles from Africa, and that she is his nurse, not Alex. Hemingway does not return to "reality." In full psychosis, he believes that his head has become the head of the Sacred Mammal. As the Kikuyo legend promised, the Sacred Mammal is avenged:

> I did not stop frightening myself: shotgun resting on my shoulder, pupil centered behind the spyhole, finger firmly on the trigger. In less than five yards, I shoot against the globulose eye, in the exact moment that its large head and tusks were coming up the wall of the window. It reeled to one side like a sinking ship, its bloody pupil looking at me with the terror of agony. I loaded the gun again, but I understand that a lucky shot is not necessary. In that instant, control of my movements gone, I feel that my own body, hawsters loose, is floating without connections.
>
> (No me dejo amedrentar: la carabina apoyada en el hombro, la pupila centrada detrás de la mirilla, el dedo firme sobre el gatillo. A menos de cinco yardas, disparo contra el ojo globuloso, en el momento exacto en que su cabezota y los colmillos alcanzaban el muro de la ventana. Se tambalea hacia un lado como barco que se hunde, la pupila sangriente mirándome con el espanto de la agonía. Vuelvo a cargar el arma, pero comprendo que no es necesario un tiro de gracia. En este instante, perdido el control de mis movimientos, siendo que mi propio cuerpo, sueltas las amarras, flota sin las ataduras.) (*Hemingway*, 341–42)

For this Afro-Colombian author, Hemingway's fascination with death by means of suicide is equated to the fulfillment of African superstition. As his spirit floats into the abyss, Hemingway glides toward his destiny: death, willfully chosen. Zapata Olivella attributes the tragic death of his protagonist to delirium resulting from the author conspiring against the laws of nature in his quest for the Sacred Mammal.

In his *Narrating the Past*, David Herzberger discusses the concept of "literary scumbling," which applies to certain novels involving the Civil War in Spain. Herzberger asserts that "literary scumbling" allows fiction and history to coexist without compromising one another. Such a novelistic paradigm is applicable to *Hemingway*. The text consists of countless references to historical events and real people who were a part of Hemingway's life. But the text's most important trait is Zapata Olivella's use of African mythology and traditions. The African influence is so profound that the author provides a glossary listing terminology and dialectic idioms particular to Kenya. African traditions abound. Episodes of drums calling the clan, warning against the arrival of outsiders, and celebrating tribal rituals are frequent. The importance of the elders in African cosmology reverberates across a number of episodes. Moreover, in one chapter, "Primero fue Africa" (Africa came first), Africa is positioned as the cradle of civilization. As Antoñete, Renata, Hemingway, and the tribesmen who accompany them sit around the fire, Antoñete ponders the origin of the species. He states that some of the earliest paleontological findings were encountered in Kenya, giving rise to the hypothesis that Africa is the origin of human existence. Upon beholding the symbiosis of the Kikuyo and nature, Hemingway agrees: "Astonished, I realized that Africa really had been the cradle of all human races." (Comprendí maravillado que Africa realmente había sido la cuna de todas las razas humanas. *Hemingway*, 62) These origins are an important element of African mythology. The African gods, it is believed, breathed life into humankind, bringing forth their existence. In one myth, the god Ngai sent his messenger to procreate with women, thus beginning dynasties of warriors, elders, troubadours, and musicians:

> The first fabulist of Kikuyo mythology, amazed before the whiteness of the Valley of Clarity, had the conviction that the Creator God of the Universe had to have the earthly bed there for resting and surprising himself with his own grandeur. They say that Ol-le-Mweiya, the messenger of Ngai, set foot first on the soil of Kenya in order to procreate with the women and found the dynasty of warriors, elders, troubadours and musicians all of whom are repositories of his wisdom.
>
> (El primer fabulador de la mitología kikuyo, asombrado ante la blancura del Valle de la Claridad, tuvo la convicción de que el Dios creador del Universo debía tener allí el lecho terrenal donde reposar y sorprenderse de su propia grandeza. Cuentan que Ol-le-Mweiya, el mensajero de Ngai, pisó aquí por primera la tierra de Kenia para procrear con las mujeres y fundar la dinastía de los guerreros, ancianos, trovadores y músicos, de todos aquéllos que son depositarios de su sabiduría.) (*Hemingway*, 261)

Additionally, proverbs offer guidance and wisdom for living life, loving, rearing a family, and regarding others. Kamau Johnstone, Kikuyo leader of the Mau-Mau and guide to the explorers, discusses the metaphysical mythology of human destiny and the labyrinthine nature of life:

Men are accompanied by two shadows—he had confessed to me—a visible one that always surrounds us when we swim lost in the light, sure reference that we are in some place accompanied by our ancestors: and the other invisible, that can only see and feel itself with the transcendent eyes of mystery; the shade that brings us destiny, long future crossings in our descent.

(A los hombres nos acompañan dos sombras—me había confesado—la visible que siempre nos rodea cuando nadamos perdidos en la luz, referencia segura de que estamos en algún lugar acompañados de nuestros Ancestros; y otra invisible, la que sólo puede verse y sentirse con el ojo trascendente del misterio: la sombra que nos depara el destino, los pasos futuros, prolongados en nuestra descendencia.) (*Hemingway*, 185–86)

The ontological and cosmological codes embedded in the representation of the two shadows demonstrate humankind's longing to unfold the hidden dual meanings manifested in nature. African mythology relies on the spirit world inhabited by visionary ancestors who provide guidance. In the text, the ancestors and nature provide answers to the existential riddles that plague humankind.

Hemingway is one of Zapata Olivella's best works of fiction. Like *Tierra mojada* and other works, *Hemingway* narrates the navigation of humankind within a specific environment. In this arena, two distinct groups intersect with nature. Africans coexist with nature while Hemingway and his entourage try to vanquish it. *Hemingway* is very similar in form and content to *Changó*. Africa, her traditions, people, and mythologies are prevalent in both texts. Africanized mythologies relating the origin of the universe are explored in both. Finally, multiple narrators, nonchronological narration, flashbacks, and interior monologues characterize both *Changó* and *Hemingway*. *Hemingway*, like other works by Zapata Olivella, offers readers a work that exhibits a mastery of the art of storytelling, displays a profound understanding of the life and works of Ernest Hemingway, and provides an in-depth familiarity with African cultural traditions.

Conclusion

The Darkening of Latin American Literature

The history of colonization, slavery, and migration of groups of people to the Americas has created a cultural configuration wherein it is
difficult to identify a monolithic populace. Miscegenation in América Latina results in the creation of a multiethnic human subject, one incorporating the history of many peoples who have all come to identify Latin
America as *la patria*. This message resonates throughout the bound
pages of Manuel Zapata Olivella's works and motivates this analysis. This
author chooses to give voice and visibility to the varied representations
of Latin Americans that are "hushed" or stereotypically exploited in literature. His corpus of literary and scholarly works reveals the distressed
lives of the New World's economically disadvantaged. Additionally, as
he matures as a writer, his messages become more political, inciting a
greater understanding of the historical challenges of the poor and those
of African ancestry in the Americas and the Diaspora at large.

As evidenced in chapter one, Manuel Zapata Olivella's literary preoccupation in his first published work emphasizes the plight of Colombia's poor and dispossessed. *Tierra* exhibits an undaunted social realism
in portraying the complexities that plague the inhabitants of the Sinú
River Valley: the racial, social, and economic disparities that run amok
and the pathology or pathologies that engender them. Themes such as
poverty, exploitation, hunger, and race frame the genesis of Manuel
Zapata Olivella's thematic literary aesthetic in this first published work.
For the readership, Zapata Olivella presents the entrance into the coarse,
gloomy, and unpredictable world of the Correa family as they navigate
the river basin in search of "place" within the confines of nature. In this
first text, this author begins his exposé of race and the African diaspora, which thematically amplifies as his talent sharpens and his worldview expands.

Chapter 2 of this work engaged Manuel Zapata Olivella's young adult
desire to explore. The works discussed attest to his longing to expand his

126

worldview. In so doing, his published "travelogues" do more than relate his adventures as a wandering border-crosser in the Americas. They engage the readership in a provocative exploration of American blackness. *Pasión* and *He visto* represent a continuum in the development of Zapata Olivella's literary discourse on the African diaspora. Revealed is the essentialist racism commonly displayed throughout the Americas toward people of African decent, including Mexicans. Neocolonial racist ideology and attitude make for cultural experiences marred by vilification, agitation, and exploitation as the narrative setting of the texts shifts from Colombia to New York City. Implicated as the instigator of racism "American-style" is the United States as her racist dogma is revealed throughout South, Central, and North America, not to exclude Mexico. *Pasión* and *He visto* enable the author's preoccupation with connecting the mid-twentieth-century history of the Americas in order to reveal the present-day circumstance as it relates to the social, economic, and political plight of blacks in disparate New World spaces. These two texts manifest Zapata Olivella's experienced reality as he witnesses the hardships of blacks. In addition, they provide a platform for the author as he probes deeper into the darkening of Latin American literature by producing works where the lives and travail of people of African ancestry are brought center stage. Both subjects and spaces are "darkened" in order to expose social realities, thus charting a new narrative course for the fiction of this Afro-Colombian author with all eyes on the greater Americas.

Clearly, the 1950s and 1960s represented tumultuous times in the history of Colombia. The literary production of Manuel Zapata Olivella plays out this historical movement novelistically. Violence, protest, rage, and resistance emerge as major themes in the works presented in chapter 3 of this analysis. *La Calle 10*, *En Chimá*, and *Chambacú* are emblematic of the realities experienced in Colombia as characters portray the social hardships and fight to survive and even advance. Characters emerge beaten by their literary realities as they confront oligarchy in order to exercise voice and agency. In *La Calle 10*, despairing characters surface as they scavenge through the spoils of Tenth Street in search of relief from the harsh reality of their existence. Mamatoco and Tamayo, among others, rise as martyrs for social justice. The chaos and filth of Tenth Street symbolize the political and social status of Colombia.

En Chimá presents the plight of a community in its fight for religious freedom. The text manipulates the travails of a largely bucolic community whose political power is hegemonic in order. In their attempt to self-govern, the people choose the most undesirable member of their depressed clan, an invalid, to become a symbolic metaphor of their disempowerment and desire to overcome. Zapata Olivella manipulates the characters in order to express his growing preoccupation with social protest. With this text the author demonstrates the power of the people to confront orthodoxy and overcome it. Cultural survival is another major component of the text. Placed in dichotomous opposition are official cultural institutions and popular practices and beliefs of the people. The invalid, Domingo Vidal, the symbol of their protest, denominates the will of a people to triumph over the socially oppressive forces of the establishment, which in this case is the Catholic Church. Hence, the end result is a narrative discourse of hope, survival, and the continuance of liberation ideology that marks the literary aesthetic of Zapata Olivella as similar strategies are employed in subsequent texts, like *Chambacú*. However, *Chambacú* places the reader in the middle of a Colombian ghetto as the strife and challenges of the people are exploited narratively.

In *Chambacú*, as in *En Chimá*, violence erupts that can be viewed as a mimetic gaze of Colombian aggression. Political and social literary protests reflect the actual disturbance in Colombia at the time. *Chambacú* advances the author's preoccupation with narrating blackness and the less than desirable social condition under which black people in Latin America have had to exist. Unlike in previous works by Zapata Olivella, race and ethnicity are not dubiously manifested in the text. Blackness is solidly affirmed by the narrative voice as is the demographic and racial inscription of the nuclear family that is centered in the novel. *Chambacú* is the author's purposed reshifting of the literary paradigm through de-marginalizing the concerns of Colombian blacks as their complaints, struggles, and protest speak from the position of the center. Circumscribing the black-constructed nucleus are the hegemonic impositions of the elite society, the invested interest of the United States, and the devastation of the Korean War in the lives of the inhabitants of Chambacú.

Manuel Zapata Olivella, as presented in chapter 4, skillfully exploits the theme of the African diaspora in *Changó*. With this text, the author synthesizes his discourses, both narrative and expository, on Africa and Africanized subjects in the New World. This text begins by placing Africa in the center of creationist thought and moves forward exposing the realities of her offspring in South America, the Caribbean, and North

America, principally the United States. The umbilical connection with the continent is inseparable as the richness of her cultural traditions is inherent in the lives of those brought forth in the novel. That which attests to the mastery of the craft of writing is Manuel Zapata Olivella's sculpturing of the work. As I indicated, this work is an exemplary example of the postmodern text. Africa is concentrically at the heart of the text as she is constructed through the narrative manipulation of time, space, and metafiction. Because of its narrative strategy of displacing, decentering, repositioning, literary self-reflection, and historicizing, *Changó* fulfills and exceeds what Linda Hutcheon considers an important theoretical component of postmodernism: historiographic metafiction.

Chapter 5 of this study presented a trilogy of texts that best represent Manuel Zapata Olivella's preoccupation with race-ethnicity in the Americas. *Levántate, Changó* and *Las claves* chronicle the history of this geographical space as the classification of people is contested due to miscegenation and racism. Zapata Olivella speaks of a tri-ethnic Latin American whose bloodline represents the story of the indigenous inhabitants, the European invaders and the enslaved Africans. Important to the many observations made by this author on race and ethnic-racial classification in the Americas is the role that racism and racist ideology played in shaping the ideology. Historical rape is implicated as a major contributor to the degree of racial mixing. Zapata Olivella's concern is personalized as his own ancestry, which he views as the progenitor of his query, is implicated. He also sees the impact of racism as it has caused many Latin Americans to reject their African blood as a result of historical vilification of that which is associated with Africa. The author's concluding message as presented in the three discussed works is self-celebration through accepting all of oneself and embracing all parts of one's ethnic-racial background.

The final chapter explored the mysteries of Africa and her cosmology as brought forth in *Hemingway*. *Hemingway* is Zapata Olivella's final published fictional work. Like *Changó*, it centers Africa and her rich cultural traditions. However, unlike in *Changó*, the vast terrain of Kenya is the principal narrative setting. Through rendering his own fictional account of the life of one of the most provocative and adventurous writers of American fiction, Ernest Hemingway, Zapata Olivella exploits Hemingway's reputation as an adventurer and writer in this work. The author places Hemingway on the mountains of Kenya, engaged in safari in order to write an impulsive work that has as its major theme the mysteries of Africa. African terrain, tribal peoples, myths, superstitions, and the continent's natural coarseness enmesh creating a work that places the reader in dialogue with the aforementioned in Zapata Olivella's attempt to present his rationale for the lunacy of Ernest Hemingway. This novel is inherently "African" and demystifies Hemingway as the great conqueror by presenting Africa as too vast an entity for Hemingway's comprehension. It is the latter that ultimately leads to Hemingway's courtship with suicide and his death. The object of Hemingway's hunt, the Sacred Mammal, becomes a symbolic metaphor in the text of all that Africa represents: vastness, mystery, nature, universal secrets, total mental-emotional consumption, and death.

For years, literature has represented Latin American culture as a monolithic entity, a reflection of the North American concept of "melting pot." However, this amalgam has undergone a hyperbolic sense of cultural "whitening" and ethnic suppression. Latin Americans have exaggerated and encouraged their "Hispanic" selves in order to suppress indigenous and African traits. In so doing, a mental state of (re)construction has occurred whereby selective amnesia facilitates the disappearance of integral parts of themselves. This self-selected identity continues to plague Latin America into the new millennium. Cultural and ethnic whitening in Latin America has caused many Latin Americans to reject and deny certain aspects of their ethnic history. This phenomenon is tantamount to the literary strategy of Manuel Zapata Olivella. The texts under review in this investigation in some form or another engage Latin American "whitening" or this concept in a more global context as whitening in terms of the relationship between Europe and Africa.

Literary "whitening" in Latin America continues to dictate the discourse of many texts. Only cursory references to indigenous populations and Africans can be found in many texts heavily steeped in Spanish influences. The phenotypic and cultural markers that compete with or overshadow Spanish ones become invisible and inconsequential to self-identity construction. Images presented in literary works often confirm the stereotype that the indigenous and African traits are less desirable than Hispanic influences, a point that Zapata Olivella develops more lucidly in his expository writings.

In summation, very few writers have dared to become iconoclasts, to venture beyond the prescribed racial and ethnic norms of traditional representation. Some, however, have attempted to be more inclusive.

These authors are challenging the concept of canonicity in Latin American literature. Manuel Zapata Olivella, Afro-Colombian writer, essayist, folklorist, political activist, and dramatist, is one of the most vocal opponents of the dominant literary ideology. He insists on portraying in fiction the multiple realities that exist in Latin America, on ensuring that "darkness is brought to the light." This cliché by no means condones literary whitening. Zapata Olivella refutes contemporary prejudices by "literary blackening," by uncovering buried realities of the black experience. In his counterargumentative approach, he does not exclude representations of the pluralism that exists in the global world. He embellishes upon the palette that as been used to paint the Latin American, ensuring that a major undertone is black(ness). Metaphorically, his texts journey through a prism that reveals the components of white, yellow, and brown, ultimately leading to black. Such "coloring" is emblematic of his ideology of postcolonial tri-ethnicity.

Manuel Zapata Olivella's work can be viewed as regionalist, modernist, and postmodernist due to the longevity of his career and the quality of his writing. What is unique about this author is his innovative treatment of common themes found in Latin American literature; his constant, unyielding, and unapologetic focus on black and indigenous experiences in Spanish America; and his preoccupation with the commonalties linking all those affected by the African diaspora experience. Zapata Olivella supports a global perspective on blackness, and he challenges his readers to broaden the horizons of their understanding of the African diaspora. He is one of the most versatile writers of Latin American literature. Few other writers can boast his literary range or match the quality of production. He is an accomplished novelist, essayist, dramatist, and short story writer. His literary strategies encompass novelistic techniques associated with both modernist and postmodernist fiction. Additionally, his eclectic literary style and his constant focus on the Afro-Hispanic experience give Manuel Zapata Olivella's work a unique and innovative quality that distinguishes him from the typical Spanish American writer.

Finally, racial/ethnic identity and identification is one of the principal emphases for this writer of mixed ancestry. As future scholars encounter his intellectual contributions, it is the hope that more of them will begin to appreciate the incredible talent of this highly gifted writer. Then maybe Manuel Zapata Olivella's writing will be given long-deserved critical attention and his place as a major figure in Latin American literature assured.

BIBLIOGRAPHY

WORKS BY MANUEL ZAPATA OLIVELLA

Zapata Olivella, Manuel. *El árbol brujo de la libertad: Africa en Colombia— orígenes, transculturación, presencia, ensayo histórico-mítico.* Buenaventura-Valle: Universidad del Pacífico, 2002.

———. *La Calle 10.* Bogotá: Ediciones Casa de la Cultura, 1960; Bogotá: Prolibros, 1986.

———. *Chambacú, corral de negros.* Medellín: Editorial Bedout, 1967; Bogotá: Rei Andes, 1990.

———. *Changó, el gran putas.* Bogotá: Editorial la Oveja Negra, 1983; Bogotá: Rei Andes Ltd., 1992.

———. *China 6 a.m.* Bogotá: Ediciones S.L.B., 1954.

———. *Las claves mágicas de América.* Bogotá: Plaza & Janés, 1989.

———. *Corral de negros.* Havana: Casa de las Américas, 1962.

———. *Detrás del rostro.* Bogotá: Editorial Revista Colombiana, 1963.

———. *En Chimá nace un santo.* Barcelona: Seix Barral, 1963.

———. *El folclor en los puertos colombianos.* Bogotá: Puertos de Colombia. 1977.

———. *El fusilamiento del diablo.* Bogotá: Plaza & Janés, 1986.

———. *He visto la noche.* Bogotá: Editorial Los Andes, 1953; San Rafael: Impresa Nacional de Cuba, 1962.

———. *He visto la noche: las raíces de la furia negra.* Medellín: Editorial Bedout, 1969.

———. *Hemingway, el cazador de la muerte.* Bogotá: Arango Editores, 1993.

———. *El hombre colombiano: con un resumen en inglés al final.* Bogotá: Canal Ramírez-Antares, 1974.

———. *Hotel de vagabundos: teatro.* Bogotá: Ediciones Espiral, 1955.

———. *Letras nacionales, numero cero.* Bogotá: 1965.

———. *¡Levántate mulato! por mi raza hablará el espiritu.* Bogotá: Rei Andes, 1990.

———. *Nuestra voz: aportes del habla popular latinoamericano al idioma español.* Bogotá: Ecoe, 1987.

———. *Pasión vagabunda: relatos.* Bogotá: Editorial Santafé, 1949; Bogotá: Ministerio de Cultura, 2000.

133

————. *¿Quién dió el fusil a Oswald? y otros cuentos.* Bogotá: Editorial Revista Colombiana, 1967.

————. *La rebelión de los genes.* Bogotá: Altamir, 1997.

————. *El subtrato psicoafrictivo y recreador del negro en el castellano hispanoamericano.* Bogotá: Banco de la República, 1980.

————. *Tierra mojada.* Bogotá: Ediciones Espiral, 1947; Madrid: Editorial Bullon, 1964; Medellín: Editorial Bedout, 1972.

Zapata Olivella, Manuel, et al. *Tradición oral y conducta en Córdoba: estudio investigativo elaborado para la División de Desarrollo Social Campesina del Incora.* Bogotá: Subgerencia de Desarrollo Agricola, División de Desarrollo Social Campesino, 1972.

Zapata Olivella, Manuel, and Nero López Meza. *Nero: la cámara trashumante.* Bogotá: Ministerio de Cultura, 1998.

Zapata Olivella, Manuel, and Patrick D. Smith. *Misto anheliv: povist'.* Kyîv: Modol', 1986.

Zapata Olivella, Manuel, and Henry Gonzaléz Torres. *Fábulas de Tamalameque.* Bogotá: Rei Andes, 1990.

WORKS IN TRANSLATION

Zapata Olivella, Manuel. *Tierra mojada.* English. Madrid: Editorial Bullon, 1964.

————. *Chambacu, Black Slum.* Translated by Jonathan Tittler. Pittsburgh: Latin American Literary Review Press, 1989.

————. *Changó, de sacré dieu.* Translated by Dorita Nouhaud. Paris: Miroirs, 1991.

————. *Changó, el gran putas.* Translated by Jonathan Tittler (forthcoming).

————. *Lève-toi, mulâtre l'esprit parlare a travers ma race.* Translated by Claude Bourguignon and Claude Couffon. Paris: Payot, 1987.

————. *A Saint Is Born in Chimá.* Translated by Thomas E. Kooreman. Austin: University of Texas Press, 1991.

WORKS BY OTHERS

Anillo Sarmiento, Antonio Francisco. "La novelística compremetida de Manuel Zapata Olivella." Ph.D. diss., George Washington University, 1972.

Barry, John. "Abriendo el canon para Manuel Zapata Olivella: 'Santa

Barbara, Bendita, ayúdanos a vivir.'" *Confluencia-Revista Hispánica de Cultura y Literatura* 8–9, no. 2–1 (1993): 249–55.

———. "El mestizaje triétnico en América 500 años después: La visión de Manuel Zapata Olivella." *Tres Américas: Revista Cultural* 5 (1993): 20–24.

Bogliolo, François. *La négritude et les problèmes du noir dans l'oeuvre de Manuel Zapata Olivella.* Dakar: Nouvelles Editions Africaines, 1978.

Brookshaw, Michael Anthony. "Protest, Militancy, and Revolution: The Evolution of the Afro-Hispanic Novel of the Diaspora." Ph.D. diss., University of Illinois Urbana-Champaign, 1983.

Bush, Roland E. "A Hermeneutic of Power: Manuel Zapata Olivella's *En Chimá nace un santo* and the 'Millenarian Dream.'" *CLA Journal* 44, no. 4 (2001): 480–91.

Cabral, Cristina. "*Changó, el gran putas*: El afrocentrismo estructural temático de 'Los Orígenes.'" *Afro-Hispanic Review* 20, no. 1 (2001): 79–89.

Captain, Yvonne. "Hacia su habitación propia: La mujer en Manuel Zapata Olivella." In *Literatura y cultura: Narrativa Colombia del siglo 20,* edited by María Mercedes Jaramillo et al. Bogotá: Ministerio de Cultura, 2000.

Captain-Hidalgo, Yvonne. "Conversación con el doctor Manuel Zapata Olivella, Bogotá 1980, 1983." *Afro-Hispanic Review* 4, no. 1 (1985): 26–32.

———. *The Culture of Fiction in the Works of Manuel Zapata Olivella.* Columbia: University of Missouri Press, 1993.

———. "El espacio del tiempo en Changó, el gran putas." In *Ensayos de literatura colombiana,* edited by Raymond Williams. Bogotá: Plaza & Janes, 1985.

———. "The Realm of Possible Realities: A Comparative Analysis of Selected Works by Alejo Carpentier and Manuel Zapata Olivella." Ph.D. diss., Stanford University, 1984.

Carrullo, Sylvia G. "La dialéctica hambre-agresión en *Chambacú, corral de negros.*" *Afro-Hispanic Review* 2, no. 3 (1983): 19–22.

Clemons, Brenda Frazier. "Manuel Zapata Olivella's 'Un extraño bajo mi piel': A Study of Repression." *Afro-Hispanic Review* 2, no. 3 (1983): 5–7.

Cobb, Martha K. "Redefining the Definitions of Afro-Hispanic Literature." *CLA Journal* 23 (1979): 147–59.

Cox, Timothy J. "New African Slavery Fiction in the Americas." Ph.D. diss., Pennsylvania State University, 1998.

————. *Postmodern Tales of Slavery in the America: From Alejo Carpentier to Charles Johnson.* New York: Garland Publications, 2001.

Davis, James J. "A Personal Perspective on the Humanism of Manuel Zapata Olivella." *Afro-Hispanic Review* 20, no. 1 (2001): 115–16.

Doerr, Richard Paul. "La magia como dinámica de evasión social en la novelística de Manuel Zapata Olivella." Ph.D. diss., University of Colorado–Boulder, 1973.

Edison, Thomas Wayne. "The Afro-Caribbean Novels of Resistance of Alejo Carpentier, Quince Duncan, Carlos Wilson, and Manuel Zapata Olivella." Ph.D. diss., University of Kentucky, 2002.

Espinosa, German. "Zapata Olivella, el aventurero: Prólogo de Pasión vagabunda." *Afro-Hispanic Review* 20, no. 1 (2001): 59–63.

Félicité-Maurice, Evelina. "La novella Afro-colombiana: Palacios, Rojas Herazo, Zapata Olivella, mito, mestizaje cultural y afrocentrismo costeño." Ph.D. diss., University of Colorado–Boulder, 1994.

Guicharnaud-Tollis, Michele. "*Changó, el gran putas* de Manuel Zapata Olivella, novela del espacio intermedio." In *Historia, espacio e imaginario,* edited by Jacqueline Covo. Villeneuve d'Ascq, France: PU de Septentrion, 1997.

Harris, Emmanuel Dwight. "Coloring Between the Lines: Racial Constructions in Selected Works of Contemporary Caribbean Fiction." Ph.D. diss., Washington University, 1998.

Harris, Mardella. "Entrevista con Manuel Zapata Olivella." *Afro-Hispanic Review* 19, no. 3 (1991): 59–61.

Heredia, Aida. "Figuras arquetípicas y la armonia racial en *Chambacó, corral de negros* de Manuel Zapata Olivella." *Afro-Hispanic Review* 6, no. 2 (1987): 3–8.

Jackson, Richard. "The Black Novel in America Today." *Chasqui-Revista de Literatura Latinoamericana* 16, no. 2–3 (1987): 23–36.

————. "Myth, History and Narrative Structure in Manuel Zapata Olivella's *Changó, el gran putas.*" *Revista/Review Interamericana* 13, no. 1–4 (1983): 108–119.

Jackson, Shirley Mae. "Temas principales de la novela negrista hispanoamericana en Lopez Albujar, Díaz Sanchez, Carpentier, Ortiz, y Zapata Olivella." Ph.D. diss., George Washington University, 1982.

Jackson, Stephen. "Los de abajo rechazan al adversario tripartido: la lucha contra la iglesia, la oligarquía y el ejército en tres novellas de

Manuel Zapata Olivella." Masters Thesis. San Diego State University, 1997.

Kooreman, Thomas E. "Integración artística de la protesta social en las novelas de Manuel Zapata Olivella." *Afro-Hispanic Review* 6, no. 1 (1987): 27–30.

———. "*Pasión vagabunda*, comienzo de una creación ficcionesa." *Afro-Hispanic Review* 8, no. 3 (1989): 3–6.

———. "Translating *En Chimá nace un santo*." *Afro-Hispanic Review* 10, no. 3 (1991): 33–36.

Krakusin, Margarita. "Conversación informal con Manuel Zapata Olivella." *Afro-Hispanic Review* 20, no. 1 (2001): 15–28.

Lewis, Marvin A. "*En Chimá nace un santo:* Myth and Violence." *Kentucky Romance Quarterly* 24 (1978): 145–51.

———. "Manuel Zapata Olivella and the Art of Autobiography." In *Colombia en el contexto latinoamericano*, edited by Myriam Luque. Bogotá: Instituto Caro y Cuervo, 1997.

———. *Treading the Ebony Path: Ideology and Violence in Contemporary Afro-Colombian Prose Fiction*. Columbia: University of Missouri Press, 1987.

———. "Violencia y resistencia: Una perspectiva literaria afrocolombiana." *Revista de Estudios Colombianos* 6 (1989): 15–20.

Luca, Dina Carmela de. "La creación de la identidad autobiográfica hispanoamericana, 1980–1994." Ph.D. diss., University of Missouri–Columbia, 1997.

———. "La práctica autobiográfica de Manuel Zapata Olivella en *Levántate mulato! 'Por mi raza hablará el gran espiritu.'*" *Afro-Hispanic Review* 20, no. 1 (2001): 43–54.

Megenney, William W. "Time and Space: Africa and America in Manuel Zapata Olivella's *Changó, el gran putas*." In *Studies in Honor of Myron Lichtblau*, edited by Fernando Burgos. Newark: Juan de la Cuesta, 2000.

Mose, Kenrick E. A. "*Changó, el gran putas* y el negro en la novelística del colombiano Manuel Zapata Olivella." *Afro-Hispanic Review* 7, no. 1–3 (1988): 45–48.

Muñoz, Alejandra Rengifo. "Poscolonialidad e identidad en Manuel Zapata Olivella, Maryse Conde y Mayra Montero." Ph.D. diss., University of Kentucky, 1999.

Ortiz, Lucía. "La obra de Manuel Zapata Olivella: Raza, poética, y sociedad." *Afro-Hispanic Review* 20, no. 1 (2001): 29–35.

Ossa, Luisa. "*Changó, el gran putas:* Afrocentric Discourse." *Monographic Review/Revista Monográfica* 15 (1999): 248–61.

Porto, Lito E. "Claroscuros: El mestizaje cromático, telúrico y racial en *Chambacú, corral de negros.*" *Afro-Hispanic Review* 19, no. 2 (2000): 59– 69.

Prescott, Laurence E. "Afro-Norteamerica en los escritos de viaje de Manuel Zapata Olivella: Hacia los origenes de *He visto la noche.*" *Afro-Hispanic Review* 20, no. 1(2001): 55–58.

Quintero, Ciro Alfonso. *Filosofía antropológica y cultural en el pensamiento de Manuel Zapata Olivella.* Quito: Curumaní-César-Colombia: Ediciones Abya-Yala; Casa de la Cultura Curumaní-César-Colombia, 1998.

Rengifo, Alejandra. "Marx, Garvey y Gaitán: Palimpsesto ideológico en *Chambacú, corral de negros.*" *Afro-Hispanic Review* 20, no. 1 (2001): 36–42.

Smart, Ian. "*Changó, el gran putas* as Liberation Literature." *CLA Journal* 35, no. 1 (1991): 15–30.

Tillis, Antonio Dwayne. "*Changó, el gran putas:* A Postmodern Historiographic Metafictional Text." *Afro-Hispanic Review* 20, no. 1 (2001): 96–103.

———. "*Changó, el gran putas:* A Postmodern Historiographic Metafictional Text." *Afro-Hispanic Review* special edition 21, no. 1–2 (2002): 171–78.

———. "La creación de una cultura nacional negra en *Nochebuena negra* de Juan Pablo Sojo y en *Chambacú, corral de negros* de Manuel Zapata Olivella." *PALARA* 5 (2001): 63–71.

———. "Manuel Zapata Olivella: From Regionalism to Post-colonialism." Ph.D. diss., University of Missouri–Columbia, 2000.

Tittler, Jonathan. "Catching the Spirit: *Changó, el gran putas* in English Translation." *Afro-Hispanic Review* 20, no. 1 (2001): 73–78.

Vassar, Uchenna Pamela. "Nationalism and the African Worldview in *Changó, el gran putas.*" Ph.D. diss., University of North Carolina–Chapel Hill, 2002.

Young, Stephanie. "In Pursuit of the Word: Marianismo and Melancolia in *En Chimá nace un santo.*" *PALARA* 3 (1999): 100–109.

Zapata Olivella, Manuel. "*Hemingway, el cazador de la muerte:* Kenya en la novela de un afrocolombiano." *PALARA* 2 (1998): 17–29.

———. "Los ancestros combatientes: Una saga afro-norteamericana." *Afro-Hispanic Review* 10, no. 3 (1991): 51–58.

Zoggyie, Haakayoo. "Lengua e identidad en *Changó, el gran putas,* de

Manuel Zapata Olivella." *Afro-Hispanic Review* 20, no. 1 (2001): 90–95.

———. "The Poetics of Disalienation in the Novelistic Work of Manuel Zapata Olivella (Colombia) and Carlos Guillermo Wilson." Ph.D. diss., University of Cincinnati, 1999.

———. *In Search of the Fathers: The Poetic Disalienation in the Narrative of Two Contemporary Afro-Hispanic Writers.* New Orleans: University Press of the South, 2003.

INDEX

ABOUT THE AUTHOR

Antonio D. Tillis is Assistant Professor of Foreign Languages and Literatures and African American Studies at Purdue University.